The Obstacles to Peace

Kenneth Wapnick

Foundation for "A.C.I.M."
RD #2, Box 71
Roscoe, NY 12776
(607) 498-4116

ISBN: 0-933291-05-1

CONTENTS

PREFACE 1
INTRODUCTION TO THE OBSTACLES
   TO PEACE 3

PART I: THE FIRST OBSTACLE
The Desire to Get Rid of It 15
The Attraction of Guilt (Chart A) 42

PART II: THE SECOND OBSTACLE
The Belief the Body is Valuable for
   What It Offers 71
The Attraction of Pain 91

PART III: THE THIRD OBSTACLE
The Attraction of Death (beg.) 119
"Ideas leave not their source." 125
"There is one life, and that
   I share with God." ...., 127
The Attraction of Death (concl.) 137
The Incorruptible Body 138
Chart B 159

PART IV: THE FOURTH OBSTACLE
The Fear of God 165
The Lifting of the Veil (beg.) 182
The Fear of Redemption 184
The Fear to Look Within 208
Looking Within 213
The Closing of the Gap 218
The Lifting of the Veil (cont.) 226
The Savior's Vision 250
The Lifting of the Veil (concl.) 273

APPENDIX
Chart A 294
Chart B 295

PREFACE

In 1985 I conducted a series of small classes at the Teaching and Healing Center in Crompond, New York. These covered different themes of *A Course in Miracles*, and each class consisted of my exegetically going through various sections line by line, in an informal setting that allowed for questions and discussion. The classes were taped, and cassette albums of these classes are available from the Foundation for "A Course in Miracles."

The present book was based on a series of classes given on "The Obstacles to Peace," a set of eight sections in Chapter 19 that together present all of the important themes of the Course. For this reason, not to mention the power and beauty of their language, these sections have from the beginning remained one of my favorite parts of the Course.

The book was prepared in the following way: The six cassette tapes from the class were first transcribed, and then gone over carefully by my wife Gloria who edited out material that, while meaningful in the original setting, seemed extraneous in written form. Stylistic redundancies and awkwardnesses of expression were also smoothed out. In many places additional material was added where it seemed necessary to explicate the points being made. Gloria and I then went through the entire manuscript together, following the same procedure. We hope that the finished product retains the spontaneity and informality of the class, as well as being a well-written book that will further understanding of these important sections in particular, and of the Course's thought system in general.

I should like to express my gratitude to the members of the class — Marjorie and Steve Darraugh, Dave Hunt, Rosemarie LoSasso, Gloria Wapnick — for their supportive and helpful participation. Without their comments and questions these tape sets and books would have been impossible. I am very grateful to Rosemarie for her careful reading of the finished manuscript and, above all, to Gloria for her painstaking editorial work in preserving the fidelity to Jesus' message in the Course, at the same time ensuring the readability of the book.

INTRODUCTION TO
THE OBSTACLES TO PEACE

There is no better group of sections than "The Obstacles to Peace" in the Course since it gives such a wonderful summary of the Course's basic teaching. These sections tie together all of the major themes of the Course from the metaphysical theme of how God did not create the world and the body to the practical teachings of guilt and projection, and their undoing through forgiveness. There are also some very beautiful passages where Jesus speaks of himself and the projections that were made on him.

We begin with the introduction to "The Obstacles to Peace" on page 379. I will place the four obstacles in their setting in the text, give a brief overview of what they are, and then we will go through them line by line.

Chapter 18 ends by talking about peace and how we will find it in the "real world," where it awaits us. The opening sections of Chapter 19 also talk about peace. They are followed by two sections, "The Unreality of Sin" and "Sin vs. Error," which talk about sin. We shall return to this topic later when we discuss how the various ego obstacles we throw up interfere with our knowing the peace of God in this world. So the idea, as always with the Course, is to help us understand what the obstacles are so that we can ask the Holy Spirit to remove them. Our natural state in this

3

world is being in our "right mind," thus letting the peace of the Holy Spirit extend through us to embrace all of us as one family.

As peace extends from deep inside yourself to embrace all the Sonship and give it rest, it will encounter many obstacles. Some of them you will try to impose. Others will seem to arise from elsewhere; from your brothers, and from various aspects of the world outside.

So the natural state is for this peace of God, given us through the Holy Spirit, to embrace all of us in that peace. And then there will be things that we will do that will interfere with that. What is being talked about here is heads and tails of the same coin. Some of the obstacles will be things that we will identify as our doing, while others would be felt as coming from other people, or various aspects in the world outside of us — all of which deal with our bodies. In other words, we feel as if we are being victimized by the various aspects of the world.

Yet peace will gently cover them, extending past completely unencumbered.

The idea is that the obstacles which seem to be so solid and so real are nothing if we let peace flow right through them. This same idea occurs in Chapter 18 where the text speaks about the "clouds of guilt" that seem to be impenetrable, but actually are nothing more than insubstantial clouds that we can pass through.

4

The extension of the Holy Spirit's purpose from your relationship to others, to bring them gently in, will quietly extend to every aspect of your lives, surrounding both of you with glowing happiness and the calm awareness of complete protection.

No one could argue with that as a goal. Here again is the central idea that peace and the Holy Spirit's purpose occur through the relationship that we had made special and unholy, but now they become healed and holy by our allowing the Holy Spirit to love through us in gentleness, embracing us in all our relationships and bringing us joy.

And you will carry its message of love and safety in freedom to everyone who draws nigh unto your temple, where healing waits for him.

This is a reference to the section which comes later in Chapter 20, "The Temple of the Holy Spirit," which says that the Holy Spirit's temple is a relationship. Our holy relationships are what allow us to draw close to the Holy Spirit and to Jesus. As we will see, Jesus will talk about this in the first obstacle. The love we feel from Jesus or the Holy Spirit in that relationship, again, attracts other people. Furthermore, the Course teaches that when the teacher is ready the pupil appears. The love and life of Christ in us, which we allow to radiate through us because of our forgiveness, then attracts other people. Many times the people this love attracts may try to attack us as they did with Jesus, for love will make them fearful as we shall discuss later. Yet it is important to remember that they are calling out for help.

You will not wait to give him this, for you will call to him and he will answer you, recognizing in your call the Call for God.

The "him" refers to "everyone." "Everyone" is a singular pronoun. It is really any brother or sister that comes to you. If you think back to that earlier section in Chapter 12, "The Circle of Atonement," this is the same idea: We undo our guilt, which is the primary obstacle to peace, through forgiveness of someone else. In the context of that relationship a light goes forth and someone will come wanting the love which is being reflected, and he or she will recognize in our call what it really is to call on the Holy Spirit. That is the Call for God that is talked about.

And you will draw him in and give him rest, as it was given you.

Once you have experienced the forgiveness of your own guilt and feel the love and peace of God, you really could not but want to extend and give that to everyone else. If you stop it then it also means you are going to be stopping Him and His love.

All this will you do. Yet the peace that already lies deeply within must first expand, and flow across the obstacles you placed before it. This will you do, for nothing undertaken with the Holy Spirit remains unfinished.

6

Here we are getting a different view of time. On the one hand Jesus is saying that we will do it, but then he is saying that there is work we have to do first. In a sense he is giving us a little pep talk, that we cannot help complete this. There is a line early on that says, "What we have begun, God Himself will complete."

PERCEPTION

You can indeed be <u>sure of nothing you see out-</u><u>side you</u>, but of this you *can* be sure: The Holy Spirit asks that you offer Him a resting place where you will rest in Him.

He is saying that we can trust nothing outside of us, because everything is an <u>illusion.</u> But the one thing in all the world we can trust is what is inside — in our <u>right mind</u>, the "resting place" — and that is the Holy Spirit. And so He is always asking that He can have a place where He can rest; the same metaphor is used in many other places. There is that lovely workbook lesson 182, "I will be still an instant and go home," where it states that the Christ in us who comes as a little child asks that He make His home in us. And there are other places where Jesus says the same thing. So he will rest in us and we will rest in him. There is also that beautiful workbook lesson, "I rest In God."

He answered you, and entered your relationship.

This is a common idea that you get throughout, especially in these middle chapters of the text where we ask the Holy Spirit to enter in our relationships through asking His help, that we forgive instead of condemn. And the minute we ask Him to enter, of course, He is there.

Would you not now return His graciousness, and enter into a relationship with Him?

In a sense He was gracious by answering our call for help and now what we answer is His call for cooperation. His call for cooperation is that we be part of His plan and extend His love to other people.

For it is He who offered your relationship the gift of holiness, without which it would have been forever impossible to appreciate your brother.
The gratitude you owe to Him He asks but that you receive for Him. And when you look with gentle graciousness upon your brother you are beholding Him.

An earlier part of this chapter talks about holiness and having faith in your brother, and this picks up on that. It is a poetic and lovely way of saying how much the Holy Spirit needs us and how much we need Him. And that what He would ask of us in terms of gratitude is that we take His love and gratitude and extend them to each other.

For you are looking where He *is*, and not apart from Him.

And where He is would be in someone whom we forgive. Minds are joined, and if we think of the Holy Spirit being in our right mind this means

that this "someone" is also in our right mind.
When I get past my wrong-minded way of looking at you, past all of my guilt and my anger, then
all that is left is the Holy Spirit in me. What I see
outside can only be what I see inside, and what I
see inside can only be what I see outside. So seeing the Holy Spirit in you has nothing to do with
seeing a little bird flying around you or seeing
some image in you. Since you are a part of me
and I am a part of you, what I am really seeing is
what I have allowed into my own mind. This is
the vision of the face of Christ, the Course's great
symbol of forgiveness. It is a vision that has nothing whatsoever to do with a perception of an ac-
tual image, such as to see the face of Jesus. Rather
the Course is talking about a shift in one's mind
that allows us to see the same physical person differently — without projections of our own belief
in sin and guilt.

**You cannot see the Holy Spirit, but you can see
your brothers truly. And the light in them will
show you all that you need to see.**

Again, the Holy Spirit is not something outside
of us. He is not something that we see with our
eyes. He is a Voice that we hear; He is an attitude
that we share; He is a way of thinking that truly
unites all people and looks beyond the projections
of our guilt that we have placed onto others. Finally, it is only with the help of the Holy Spirit
that we can pass the darkness that we have en-
shrouded others in, and see the light in them and
nothing else. In another section Jesus says that we

will see the miracles that will be done through us and we will know that we did not do them but something in us did them. And that something of course is really Someone.

When the peace in you has been extended to encompass everyone, the Holy Spirit's function here will be accomplished.

The reference here is to the "real world," when our mind is totally healed. At that point the Holy Spirit's function in our life is completed. When everyone reaches that point — the end of the carpet — that is the Second Coming, followed by the Last Judgment and God's final step. The Holy Spirit's function is to take the peace that comes from God and extend it freely without any interferences at all so that it embraces every aspect of the Sonship.

ANYONE

What need is there for seeing, then?

The only need we have for seeing now is to correct the misperceptions of the ego and to obtain the true perception of the vision of Christ. When that has been totally accomplished and no spots of darkness remain, the whole purpose of this world is finished.

When God has taken the last step Himself, the Holy Spirit will gather all the thanks and gratitude that you have offered Him, and lay them gently before His Creator in the name of His most holy Son.

Obviously this whole theme is metaphoric, but
certainly it is the same idea talked about in Chapter 5: When the Atonement is complete the Holy
Spirit will still remain, since what God creates is
eternal, and then He remains to bless all of our
creations. It is just another way of saying the
same thing.

**And the Father will accept them in His Name.
What need is there of seeing, in the presence of
His gratitude?**

This is a lovely vision of what happens when
we finally get past all the obstacles to peace. We
return in our awareness to the perfect unity of
Heaven. LOVE
Before we proceed to the first obstacle let me
say what the four obstacles are. The first three obstacles reflect different forms of attack. The first
obstacle talks specifically about attack. Thus, the
first obstacle to peace is our desire to get rid of it
by attacking other people. The second obstacle
more specifically focuses on our attack upon ourselves. It talks a great deal about the body, needs
of the body, seeing it either as an object of pleasure or pain. The third obstacle is the full extension of that attack which is death: the attraction of
death, the attraction of murder, whether we are
talking about the murder of someone else or the
murder of ourselves. So what we are really talking about in the first three obstacles to peace are
the projections of our guilt and different ways of
talking about it. Each one gets us deeper and
deeper into the ego's thought system, and leads

to the final obstacle, which is the fear of God. It is
this fear of God that causes us to continue to project our guilt onto everyone else, to attack other
people, to attack ourselves and to make death
real. All of these, as we shall see, become ways of
protecting us from what the ego interprets as
God's wrath. Each of the obstacles is in two parts.
The second section of each obstacle is commen-
tary on what the obstacle is. It is really a brilliantly
conceived set of sections.

PART 1:
THE FIRST OBSTACLE

The First Obstacle:
The Desire to Get Rid of It

The first obstacle to peace is the desire to get rid of it, and the "it" of course is peace. So the first obstacle is that we do not want peace. We will go on to explain that the way we demonstrate or we manifest our desire *not* to be peaceful is to attack.

NOT FORGIVE

The first obstacle that peace must flow across is your desire to get rid of it. For it cannot extend unless you keep it. You are the center from which it radiates outward, to call the others in.

This emphasizes the choice that we make. We either choose to keep the peace or we choose to give it away by attacking other people.

You are its home; its tranquil dwelling place from which it gently reaches out, but never leaving you.

Again, the "its" is peace. What we give we also receive, since ideas leave not their source, a concept we shall discuss in more depth later on. As we give peace to other people it remains within us. This reflects the process of extension in Heaven that cannot be understood if we think of it from a spatial point of view. God extends His Love, yet His Love is retained within Him; and since we are His Love then we are retained within Him as well.

If you would make it homeless, how can it abide within the Son of God? If it would spread across the whole creation, it must begin with you, and from you reach to everyone who calls, and bring him rest by joining you.

Let us go back to that same idea of resting in God within our mind. What this means, then, is that if we want to obscure the peace that is in us, and fight or defend against it, all we have to do is to decide not to extend peace. That automatically blocks it, not only from my extending peace to you but it certainly blocks its extension from myself.

Why would you want peace homeless? What do you think that it must dispossess to dwell with you? What seems to be the cost you are so unwilling to pay?

The text does not really answer these questions here, but if we want to keep peace within ourselves then we have to give guilt away. We'll continue this in the next section, "The Attraction of Guilt." This is a little similar actually to the section on "The Laws of Chaos" in Chapter 23 which talks about the priceless pearl in our brother's body that we want. There it is even spoken about in a much more powerful way in terms of what we do with our guilt.

The little barrier of sand still stands between you and your brother. Would you reinforce it now? You are not asked to let it go for yourself alone. Christ asks it of you for Himself.

Now the little barrier of sand is really our anger and attack. I think we can understand this in two ways: First is exactly what the text is saying, that the desire to hold on to our peace or let go of our "barrier of sand" is done for Christ's sake, literally. Christ asks it of us so that He can find His home in us. In other words He cannot be at home in us unless we invite Him in. He certainly is at home in our true Self because that *is* Christ, but we have drawn a curtain around it. Secondly, as we have seen in other places in the Course, releasing our anger is being asked of us for all people. The workbook lesson "When I am healed I am not healed alone" echoes this same theme.

He would bring peace to everyone, and how can He do this except through you?

It is that same idea you find in the workbook lesson "Salvation of the world depends on me."

Would you let a little bank of sand, a wall of dust, a tiny seeming barrier, stand between your brothers and salvation?

Now the trick is when you really feel yourself angry at someone, and the fury rages up inside of you, to then think of these phrases, "a little bank of sand, a wall of dust, a tiny seeming barrier," which is another way of saying that the fury is nothing; just as "The Two Worlds" talks about the "clouds of guilt" being insubstantial, even though it seems at the moment that what you are feeling is very real.

And yet, this little remnant of attack you cherish still against each other *is* the first obstacle the peace in you encounters in its going forth. This little wall of hatred would still oppose the Will of God, and keep it limited.

To whatever extent we would choose to hate or attack someone, then at that moment peace will disappear from us. If you think about the three steps of forgiveness that I have spoken about other times, the first step of forgiveness is to say, "I am not angry at you, I am really angry at myself." In other words, you bring the guilt from outside inside so this first obstacle to peace is really the same idea. The first obstacle to peace is that we are still choosing to let this little wisp of a nothing, which is a projection of our guilt, stand between our brother and ourself. So rather than seeing it as a little wisp of nothing we see it as a solid wall of granite which then becomes the means of our justifying our anger. So in our minds we say, "This person has done something that is so terrible that I can never be friends with him or her again," or whatever form the idea takes.

The Holy Spirit's purpose rests in peace within you. Yet you are still unwilling to let it join you wholly. You still oppose the Will of God, just by a little. (Jesus is a little optimistic here.) **And that little is a limit you would place upon the whole. God's Will is one, not many. It has no opposition, for there is none beside it.**

This is merely repeating the same idea that

there is a part of us — and this is a choice on our part — that is unwilling to let this barrier go. That last line I read is reminiscent of the Course's earlier quoting from the Bible that there should be no other gods before Him, which is such a famous quote. The answer is that there can be no other gods before God because there are none. It is not said as a threat or a demand. It is a simple statement of a simple fact. There can be no other God because there is no other God. All the other gods are just idols which do not exist, and this is the same idea here. To say God's Will is one, not many, is to state that our seemingly separate wills are really non-existent. Again, this is another reflection of the non-duality of the Course's system. There is only God's Will and there is nothing else. And that is why it is so important to keep in mind the basic Course premise: God did not create this world and there is nothing of Him that is in this world; moreover, everything of this world speaks of the opposite of Him.

What you would still contain behind your little barrier and keep separate from your brother seems mightier than the universe, for it would hold back the universe and its Creator. This little wall would hide the purpose of Heaven, and keep it *from* Heaven.

No matter how insignificant and trivial our guilt is, it is powerful enough within our mind to hold back Heaven, not in reality, but certainly in our experience. Later on in the text Jesus uses the image of the mouse and says how the ego seems to

19

be like a roaring lion, but in reality is just a frightened mouse that roars at the universe.

Q: Is peace the all-important object that you would still contain behind your little barrier?

A: No, that is guilt because it says that what you would still contain behind the barrier seems mightier than the universe. It is guilt that has the power within our mind to hold the universe away. It is tricky because in other places it says that peace is behind the barrier. This is not the easiest reading, to say the least.

Q: Why do we believe that guilt is mightier than God's universe?

A: Because guilt comes from the belief that we have sinned or separated ourselves from God, which means that we have attacked Him and have taken His power and misused it. Just the fact that we believe we are here in the body and the world seems to be proof that we have accomplished that. Within this world God is totally absent, which means that this world has the power to keep God away; and what keeps the world going is our guilt. By the way, here the Course is using "universe," not in the idea of the physical universe, which it sometimes does elsewhere, but rather as the universe of Christ or Heaven.

Would you thrust salvation away from the giver of salvation? For such have you become.

Now we are saying that we have taken salvation from ourselves. We are the ones who can give salvation by letting the Holy Spirit extend His love and peace to us, and we are taking it away by holding on to our anger. There are other places in the material which talk about our brother as the giver of salvation. Here the Course is talking about ourself and, of course, it does not make any difference.

Peace could no more depart from you than from God.

Again, this is another little celestial pep talk that, despite how disquieted and awful we might feel, peace is still within us because the Holy Spirit is still within us. No matter how powerful we think we are in terms of our defensive system, the ego cannot put out of our mind what God put there, which is the Holy Spirit or, in this case, peace.

Fear not this little obstacle. It cannot contain the Will of God. Peace will flow across it, and join you without hindrance. Salvation cannot be withheld from you. It is your purpose. You cannot choose apart from this.

Therefore no matter how angry we feel, no matter how wretched we feel we are, none of this can stop or change what God has ordained. Because God has given us the Holy Spirit in our mind we can never totally be insane again. In an ancient instant we became totally insane when we separated, and at that very instant the Holy Spirit was created and became part of our mind. That meant

21

there was a built-in saving factor. No matter how much we may wander away, at some point we will still choose to fulfill the Holy Spirit's purpose.

You have no purpose apart from your brother, nor apart from the one you asked the Holy Spirit to share with you.

The only purpose we have in this world is to forgive whomever it is that has to be forgiven. There is no other purpose. The purpose is not to teach the Course, not to preach the Bible, nor to become famous and amass a lot of money. The only purpose that the Holy Spirit sees in this world is the healing of God's Son. This is accomplished by simply forgiving those people whom we live with, whom we work with, grew up with, etc. Indeed, this includes all people and relationships.

The little wall will fall away so quietly beneath the wings of peace. For peace will send its messengers from you to all the world, and barriers will fall away before their coming as easily as those that you interpose will be surmounted.

Just as easily as we have set up barriers and obstacles, just as easily will they be taken from us. This foreshadows what we will talk about in the next section about the messengers of fear or the messengers of love that we send out. And if you think back to that first section in Chapter 18, ''The Substitute Reality,'' we find the exact same idea: No matter how awesome and enormous our errors and sins seem to us they are really nothing.

Like feathers in the wind they just kind of dance and whirl and fall all over the place, but they have no substance. The unsubstantial nature of all illusions is a theme you find all through the Course. Not only on Level One is the phenomenal world not real, but also on Level Two: our perceptions and judgments of hatred, attack, loss, suffering, sadness and death are all not real. When we change our mind and let the Holy Spirit in, then everything else changes accordingly.

To overcome the world is no more difficult than to surmount your little wall.

Q: That reminds me of the sentence in the middle of the page we just read: "This little wall of hatred would still oppose the Will of God." Towards the end of Chapter 3 the text states that we believe we made a will in opposition to God and that really is the devil. So what the whole thing really boils down to in that one sentence — "The little wall of hatred would still oppose the Will of God" — is the entire ego system. The thought that we have made a world in opposition to God and that opposes His Will is what is holding us back, and that is why we hold onto the hatred so much: We have to convince ourselves that this world is real because we made it.

A: Whatever it is that you make you have a vested interest in. Therefore on a larger scale we made the world and we do not want to let it go, simply because if we let it go then nothing will be left but God, and that is what frightens us. But that is all it is. The idea is so simple and yet, we leave a

23

room like this and return to our daily living and everything gets us upset. It could be the most trivial thing in the world and it will just blow everything for us. What this is saying is that no matter what it is, no matter how powerful it seems, it is nothing but a "little wall of hatred." And it *is* hatred. Certainly that is what is emphasized here; everything ends up as being hateful. Many times it is obvious to us that it is hate, but many other times it is not.

Q: Is the "little gap" that is referred to later on the same idea?

A: There it is talking about sickness in terms of the gap, the seeds of sickness are in the gap, but that is exactly the same idea. All it is is a little gap, a little wall, a speck of dust, a little barrier of sand, a cloud; it is really nothing.

Q: In terms of the way we experience it, it is really our investment in believing that this world we made is really something terrific.

A: And our investment, as you said, is because we are afraid if we give up the investment the whole world will disappear. There is a line in Chapter 13 that says, in effect, if you let all of this go you will jump into your Father's arms. And that would make us happy, but we prefer to be right.

Q: What about feelings of inadequacy and self-hatred? For example, people feel they ought to do well, but they feel intellectually inferior, cannot work or understand computers, are not good secretaries, or whatever.

A: Right, they become symbols of their own inadequacy.

Q: On Level Two how would you handle that?

A: You realize: "I am not a good secretary; I erased all the files in the computer. So what." If you look at it from the point of view of eternity what difference does it make? That is how you handle it; you realize that what is upsetting you is the interpretation you are making of what you did or what you failed to do. That is what is upsetting you. Not that you mistyped a letter, or you flunked an exam, or you pressed the wrong keys on the computer, or you answered the phone wrong or you did not do whatever it is — that is not what is upsetting you. What is upsetting you is your interpretation of it, which is: "My God, what a terrible person I am, how inadequate; what a failure I am, what a sinful person I am." That is the problem. You see, it is not the thing itself; it is the interpretation that we have placed upon it.

So if you read about something in the newspaper or hear about something on the radio, it is not the news that is upsetting you, it is the interpretation that you make of it. The interpretation would always come down to some belief that sin is real, whether it is in someone else or it is in ourselves. So the way out of it is to realize that what is upsetting me is not what I did or what others did. It is how I am looking at what they did. The Course says that perception is an interpretation, not a fact. Acceptance of this takes a lot of hard work, especially because we have all made some very powerful symbols of our guilt and our failures. The most trivial thing in the world could set us off. But then we look back on it and realize what it really is.

Another thing that is helpful is if you remember something in the past that upset you, whether it was last week, last month or last year, or when you were a child, think about the incident and realize how silly it all was. It was not silly at the time because you made a connection or interpretation that upset you. It is the connection that is the problem, not the thing itself. The whole matter boils down to a silly idea that we are no good, that we have sinned, and that we have to protect ourselves from the enormity of our sin by making up the world that seems to be outside of us. That is why we have such a strong investment in believing the world is real: It "protects" us from confronting our own sinfulness. That is why so many people can study this Course for years and just not see that it is saying God did not create this world. Because if He did create the world then psychologically we are off the hook. But if He did not create the world that means we did. What follows then is we made the whole thing up, which means it is not real, and therefore we are driven back inside of us to what we believe is real which is our sin and guilt. That is the meaning of the statement made at the end of the introduction to the text:

**This course can therefore be summed up very
simply in this way:**
Nothing real can be threatened.
Nothing unreal exists.
Herein lies the peace of God.

So the whole world then becomes a smoke
screen and a defense against having to look
within ourselves. Because if we did make up the
world and God did not, then it means it is all in
our mind and that is precisely why we have such
a tremendous investment in denying that. Or, in
the context of this section, a tremendous investment in keeping attack real.

Q: With a news broadcast of some tragic event not
only is it our interpretation, but the very words of
the news broadcaster are already the interpretation.

A: Everything is an interpretation; what news is
reported and what news is not reported. Basically
we all know that there is no objective news re-
porting. There cannot be. But there is no objective
anything. There is no objective research or sci-
ence, because it is all filtered through our perception which comes from how we choose to see
something, or our unconscious beliefs and values.
For example, consider a book such as the Course
which would seem to be the purest of any teachings that we have, certainly among the purest in
our recorded history. Yet you get totally different
perceptions of what it is saying, depending on
where people are coming from. A fundamentalist
Christian will see this as the work of the devil. We

27

see it as the work of God. How you understand the Course becomes perfectly consistent within one's particular thought system.

Q: Is it not also true, that when you look in the world for substantiation of what you feel, it is really discouraging to see how you are constantly getting this feedback that you are a failure? I know that on the unconscious level we are constantly attracting the failure in certain areas because we have made them to be symbols of failure; as in my losing my keys for the sixteenth time.

A: That is the attraction of guilt. See, the ego is slippery. For example, when you lose your keys sixteen times, your ego tells you that you are nothing but a dunce, inadequate, a failure and all that, and you are not blaming other people. You keep blaming yourself, which in one sense is true. You are the one who is losing the keys. But it does not tell you that the problem is not that you have lost the keys, but you have chosen to continue to reinforce how guilty you are, and you have chosen that form: losing your keys. Your ego is half right. You have done it. What you have really done, however, is not acting stupid by losing the keys, but rather choosing to *prove* that you are stupid by losing the keys, and that is the attraction of guilt we will get to a little later.

Q: Then the answer again is to just recognize all of this as an interpretation that I have made, and I can change my mind.

A: Right. Guilt is a very powerful feeling. The way out of it is to become aware that losing my keys sixteen times is my call for help. Then I can realize I am making the whole thing up, and the specific reason I am bringing this on myself is so I can prove that I am not any good and prove that I have sinned against God and attacked Him.

Q: What comes to mind again is the section "What is the World?" at the back of the workbook, which says that "The world was made as an attack on God." We just keep repeating this attack syndrome by attacking everything and everyone in our environment and the world. It is that rebelliousness that keeps us attacking, and it seems as if we cannot let go of it. And so we just keep propagating those same attack thoughts. So now we do not think we are attacking God consciously, because we have consciously substituted attacking everyone and everything.

A: We should realize everytime we get mildly annoyed at anyone that it is really a reflection of a much deeper unconscious thought and belief of attacking God. But the whole scenario is so repressed it seems that what we are really upset with is reality. The idea that to overcome the world is no more difficult than to surmount a little wall is saying that it is all the same thing. Again, the idea of the funnel illustrates that the outer tip of the funnel is really the exact same thing as the base of it, i.e., ideas leave not their source.

For in the miracle of your holy relationship, without this barrier, is every miracle contained.

Forgiving one person or healing one thought in our mind extends through us to heal the whole world because it is all the same thing, a projection of what is within us. So in forgiving one person and truly healing one relationship, all miracles are contained as well. To forgive truly means to let go of the guilt. And at that point the projection of that guilt into all of the different areas of our lives, whether it is our own body or other peoples' bodies — all of that will be corrected and healed, too.

There is no order of difficulty in miracles, for they are all the same.

That is why, again, it is imperative when working with this material to understand that basic metaphysical statement of the Course, i.e., the entire phenomenal physical world, all the bodies and everything that happens to the body, comes from our ego mind which is totally outside of the Mind of God. That is why every answer to every problem is the same. There is no order of difficulty in miracles.

Each is a gentle winning over from the appeal of guilt to the appeal of love. How can this fail to be accomplished, wherever it is undertaken? Guilt can raise no real barriers against it. And all that seems to stand between you must fall away because of the appeal you answered.

It cannot fail because the Holy Spirit in us insures that it succeeds. Guilt can raise seeming barriers, but it cannot raise any real barriers. If you truly answered a call for love or the appeal for love, everything else must disappear.

From you who answered, He Who answered you would call.

When we answer the Holy Spirit's call, He (the Holy Spirit) who answered us would now call to other people. It is a reciprocal process that embraces everyone. We are calling to the Holy Spirit for help; He is calling to us to hear His Voice so He can help us and other people through us; we call to our brothers; they call to us. It really is all an expression of that one basic call, and is rephrased from the Bible on page 39 of the text: "All are called but few choose to listen."

His home is in your holy relationship. Do not attempt to stand between Him and His holy purpose, for it is yours.

Later on Jesus says the exact same thing; that he stands within our holy relationship. Another major theme of the Course you find in many workbook lessons is that our will and God's are the same; in reality, not in the dream. In this world the Holy Spirit's function is to remind us of this, and that is His holy purpose.

But let Him quietly extend the miracle of your relationship to everyone contained in it as it was given.

There is a hush in Heaven, a happy expectancy, a little pause of gladness in acknowledgment of the journey's end. For Heaven knows

you well, as you know Heaven. No illusions stand between you now.

Here it is assuming that we have already chosen to get beyond this obstacle and to let the peace extend through us.

Look not upon the little wall of shadows.

This is a reference to Plato's allegory of the cave which you find in Book VII of *The Republic*. The image there is how we are all chained in the interior of the cave. We cannot look behind us to the cave's opening, where the light and sun are. Thus all we see are shadows of the people on the road passing by the mouth of the cave, yet we take the shadows to be reality. The allegory goes on to state that one of the prisoners breaks away and makes his way out into the light of the upper world. At first it hurts his eyes; he gets accustomed to it and he suddenly realizes where reality is. It is not within the cave in the shadows, but it is above and outside. He realizes that it is his function now to go back into the cave and waken his brothers and release them. Plato then states that if anyone tried to release them and lead them up, they would kill him if they could lay hands on him.

Obviously prisoners do not want to be released from the cave, which is really the ego and the world of darkness, and they would kill an enlightened person who tried to show them the way out. In the allegory Plato is referring to his teacher, Socrates, who was killed by people who did not want to hear the truth that he was teaching them.

Q: Sounds like what happened to Jesus.

A: Yes, but what this is really referring to is that we chose to look on the world as a world of shadows. And the real world, again, is a world of light; it is still the phenomenal world, yet everything and everyone is bathed in forgiveness.

The sun has risen over it. How can a shadow keep you from the sun? No more can you be kept by shadows from the light in which illusions end.

Here we can say the sun is risen over the world of shadows, which would really be the sun of forgiveness. The passage talks about just experiencing ourselves standing outside, a shadow in the sun, and then states that that really is a symbol of the shadows of our illusions; a shadow of our guilt and hatred that cannot keep us from the light of truth and the light of love.

Every miracle is but the end of an illusion. Such was the journey; such its ending. And in the goal of truth which you accepted must all illusions end.
The little insane wish to get rid of Him Whom you invited in and push Him out *must* produce conflict.

This is an important idea, which is talked about in many different places in the Course. Our natural state is to be with the Holy Spirit or Jesus, resting in peace with Them. There is a part of us that yearns for that. Whenever we choose to get angry, to attack, or to see separation in any way, then we are basically going against ourselves. That must inevitably produce conflict. It is the same idea the text discusses in the sections on specialness. In the instant when we choose to lay aside the guilt of our special relationships and to have them become holy, we will experience conflict because there is a part of us that is still holding on to guilt. As a result we can go through a period of disorientation, with a lot of conflict and pain. Remember, this is not a path of sweetness and light; it has a lot of ups and downs. As we continue to confront our own guilt and become closer and closer in touch with this conflict of God or the ego, peace or turmoil, love or murder, the tension increases. The realization occurs that part of us wants peace and happiness, yet another part of us is choosing hatred, anger and attack.

You talk to people who say that in meditation they experience a tremendous peace. But there is no excitement there, there is nothing in that; it is boring. Conflict is exciting. Right? So a part of us is tremendously attracted to conflict. You just have to look at the football or basketball games or any of the sports around; it is all competition and conflict. The greater the conflict, the greater the struggle and fighting, the greater the peak experience. The participants like it, and millions and millions of people who watch it like it, because it feeds that same idea that separation is real, and the conflict with each other is real and desirable. This then becomes the camouflage for the real conflict and separation that is our opposition to God. By holding on to it out here in the world, we

34

do not have to deal with it in our own minds.

As you look upon the world, this little wish (which is the wish to keep peace out, and the Holy Spirit out), **uprooted and floating aimlessly, can land and settle briefly upon anything, for it has no purpose now.**

So what has happened now is that we have dislodged this anger sufficiently, and it no longer has that kind of power over us. It is just floating around and can land on almost anything. This is when we will experience the most trivial things in the world as upsetting: if somebody does not look at us quite right, or our buttons get pushed when we hear about some situation.

Before the Holy Spirit entered to abide with you it seemed to have a mighty purpose (i.e., that insane wish, that wish to keep that barrier between ourselves and peace); **the fixed and unchangeable dedication to sin and its results. Now it is aimless, wandering pointlessly, causing no more than tiny interruptions in love's appeal.**

The decision to be angry and to attack people was really a decision to make sin real, because it keeps us separate. Again, this is assuming now that we are really letting go of our investment in anger.

Q: Would you elaborate on the fixed and unchangeable dedication to sin and its results?

A: This dedication to sin, of course, is the ego's,

for its very existence is dependent on our belief in the separation which *is* the definition of sin. Remember that the Course defines the ego as the thought of separation. We have seen many other times that what makes sin real to us is our experience of guilt. And since guilt always demands punishment the results of our dedication to sin must be pain, misery, suffering, sickness, death, despair, depression, anxiety, fear and terror.

This feather of a wish, this tiny illusion, this microscopic remnant of the belief in sin, is all that remains of what once seemed to be the world. It is no longer an unrelenting barrier to peace. Its pointless wandering makes its results appear to be more erratic and unpredictable than before.

Our resistance, which can feel like a granite wall, is just a feather, a tiny illusion, a microscopic remnant. Assuming that we have already chosen peace, we are at the point where we have let it go, but not totally because it is still around floating. This is reflecting the experience of getting upset over nothing. The next line is very important from a psychological point of view.

Yet what could be more unstable than a tightly organized delusional system?

Those people who are psychologically categorized as obsessive compulsives tend to be very rigid within a tightly organized system; and when we talk about a tightly organized delusional system we are talking about a full-blown paranoid system. We are not referring here to compulsivities that we all would have. Clinically it usually comes with people who are very bright. They have worked out a whole system in which, for example, the FBI is plotting against them, or the Russians are plotting against them, or everybody is plotting against them. They may be on a subway and believe everybody is talking about them, people get off because of them, or people get on the train because of them.

The more that you hold on to this paranoid thinking, the tighter the system becomes. That is because it is concealing the exact opposite underneath; that you are afraid that you are going to fall apart. This is the idea of compensation which Freud and Jung talked about in great depth; that we compensate for what is within us by doing the opposite. So if I feel that I am about to fall apart, I believe magically that by keeping everything externally perfect, I will be held together. So, people who insist everything on a desk has to be absolutely perfect, or their clothes have to be absolutely perfect, or their food has to be a certain way on a plate, exhibit this pattern. We all have certain aspects of this because the ego part of us always feels as if it is going to fall apart.

Another way of saying the same thing is that we are terrorized that God will destroy us from within, so we put a fence around the fear. Next, we have the crazy idea that by controlling every aspect of our external life we are really in control of what is inside of us. That is the meaning of the line in the text, page 334: "It is essential to realize that all defenses *do* what they would defend"; the more we hold on to those outer defenses, the more we hold on to organizing our life outside, whether it is a thought system as implied here, or a behavioral system, or both. What it really does is reinforce how fragile and unstable we are inside.

And the point is that we all have the same dynamics going on; we are all paranoid. The whole ego system is a paranoid system. It is just that certain people are far more extreme. In this sense then, we are all Hitlers. We all believe we are inadequate, and we all believe that by persecuting, or getting even, by attacking other people, or being better than other people, we will be better off. Hitler just took that dynamic and became its most powerful and extreme example. However, we all share that same idea that gives away what is underneath. The model here, therefore, is a paranoid system, but it is the ego system which we all share. Moreover, what really is unstable is the belief in attack or the belief in sin.

Its seeming stability is its pervasive weakness, which extends to everything.

Because projection makes perception — once we begin with that basic belief in sin and our having opposed God within us — everything that we perceive will be perceived through those lenses, unless we change the whole basic premise. Therefore, the more that you try to be stable the more you are reinforcing what the stability is trying to protect you *from*. Again: "Defenses do what they would defend"; and it is never enough because there is no way that we could control everything in the environment. We always have to do more and more, and things are always falling apart and getting out of control.

Q: It reminds me of the overkill argument in the nuclear defense system. For example, you talk to somebody who says, "I do not feel safe at forty overkill." It is useless to carry on a conversation because they are not going to feel safe at one hundred or at four thousand overkill.

A: Yes, it actually is the same idea. That is the paranoid system. If you really analyzed and listened to what nuclear overkill proponents are saying it has nothing to do with nuclear defense, political advantage or international concerns. It has to do with a purely individual feeling that they are fragile underneath and that they have to be protected.

Q: No amount of defense is going to help them.

A: Right, because the inner fragility gets projected out onto a larger scale. The Course urges us to make no exceptions and to generalize these principles to everything, whether you are talking about international relations or your own family, or your own personal self; they are all the same. Everything is the same. Again, if you think of the funnel: everything comes from the base of the funnel, especially the belief that we are separated from God. Everything else is seen through those eyes.

The variability the little remnant induces merely indicates its limited results.

Basically what that means is that our reactions are so variable. If we really think about it we can see in ourselves that something will not bother us one day, and the next it will really upset us. We are extremely variable in our reactions to people and to ourselves. Our attitudes are always changing. And that is·what shows us that it is not real, because God is constant, love is constant, and truth has no variations.

This final paragraph is a lovely one. Again, we find reiterated the idea of how can we take this whole thing seriously? What power does the ego have against God?

How mighty can a little feather be before the great wings of truth? Can it oppose an eagle's flight, or hinder the advance of summer? Can it interfere with the effects of summer's sun upon a garden covered by snow? See but how easily this little wisp is lifted up and carried away, never to return, and part with it in gladness, not regret. For it is nothing in itself, and stood for nothing when you had greater faith in its protection. Would you not rather greet the summer sun than fix your gaze upon a disappearing snowflake, and shiver in remembrance of the winter's cold?

A lovely paragraph indeed, with an image which is used frequently. That is all sin is: a disappearing snowflake. Just think about how insignificant a snowflake is: a little warmth and the whole thing disappears. That is all that sin, guilt and attack are. The trick again is to remember that when you are tempted to make the snowflake into a glacier; it still is nothing. It was always nothing. It says in the top line of page 382, "For it is nothing in itself, and stood for nothing when you had greater faith in its protection." Even when you believed attack could protect you, it was still nothing; it always was nothing. It stood for nothing because the ego is nothing, and yet out of that nothing we made a whole big thing.

The Attraction of Guilt (Chart A)

The attraction of guilt produces fear of love, for love would never look on guilt at all.

This section begins with a line which is one of Bill Thetford's favorites. The first half of that sentence — "The attraction of guilt produces fear of love" — is one of the Course's most central statements and reflects the basic dynamics of the ego. As long as we are guilty and choose to be guilty, our guilt demands punishment. That is a basic law of the ego — that guilt always demands and expects punishment. We ultimately believe that it is God who will punish us, because it is God whom we believe we have attacked. Therefore whenever we are guilty we must become afraid of love. And that is the meaning of that very important first phrase, "The attraction of guilt produces fear of love, for love would never look on guilt at all."

UNCONSCIOUS

UNWORTHY

What we have in this first paragraph is another kind of stylistic recurring theme in the Course where Jesus is putting forth mutually exclusive states. If we are guilty it must lead to fear. If however, we choose love, it is impossible to have any kind of fear or guilt at all. So what this means then is that our guilt then becomes afraid of love, because if we are guilty and then choose love, love would automatically banish the guilt. This then leads to the ego's attempts to justify to us its belief that love is really to be feared, because love will punish. There are two lines in one of Helen's poems that say, "Love does not crucify. It only saves. . . . God does not crucify. He merely is." The ego, of course, would teach us that love does crucify. So the ego is afraid of love because love would mean the end of the ego. Therefore the ego teaches us that love is to be feared.

It is the nature of love to look upon only the truth, for there it sees itself, with which it would unite in holy union and completion.

Love, again, could only look on the truth because there it sees a reflection of itself and, in that truth, it joins with itself. This is a theme which is picked up near the end of the section, and when we come to it I will talk about it in the context of communion. The Course's view of communion is entirely different from the traditional Christian view. So here you see a hint of what will come later on: that true communion is the union of love with love. Further, love can only look on truth which means it looks beyond the illusions of the ego. That is why the ego must be afraid of it.

As love must look past fear, so must fear see love not. For love contains the end of guilt, as surely as fear depends on it.

It is the same idea. Love and fear are mutually exclusive states. You cannot have both together. There are no grey areas here; it is one or the other, love or fear. Just as at the beginning when the Course talks about healing it says that in order for healing to occur, there must be an instant where the healer must be totally without fear. Now the healer could then choose in the next instant to be fearful again, but in that one instant of healing there will have to be an absence of fear. Similarly Jesus says at the beginning that he would come in response to a single unequivocal call, which means a call of love rather than a call of fear.

Overlooking guilt completely, it (love) **sees no fear. Being wholly without attack, it could not be afraid.**

This is reflective of another key dynamic in the ego system. When we attack someone we must automatically and inevitably believe that, because we have made attack real, we will be attacked in return; someone else must do the same thing to us. So as long as we attack we will always be afraid. And of course it is that same dynamic which is in back of the whole madness of the nuclear arms race. Each country is ultimately terrified that nuclear weapons will be used against it simply because it is amassing such an arsenal itself.

Fear is attracted to what love sees not (which would be guilt), **and each believes that what the other looks upon does not exist.**

Again, it is the theme of the mutually exclusive nature of love and fear.

Fear looks on guilt with just the same devotion that love looks on itself. And each has messengers which they send forth, and which return to

them with messages written in the language in which their going forth was asked.

Now we are going to move into what is the central theme of the section and one of the key ideas in the entire Course. The problem is never the messages that are brought back to us, the messages of all the horrors that we perceive in the world. The problem is always which is the messenger we chose first to send out into the world. If you look at Chart A, the dark point on the left is the mind which is the place of decision. It is at this point that we choose to send one of two messengers out into the world. The line that goes up is the messenger of the ego, the messengers of fear. The line on the bottom would be the messenger belonging to the Holy Spirit, the messengers of love and forgiveness. What is seen on the screen, which is the vertical line coming down on the right, is the world, which consists of all kinds of terrible witnesses to its so-called reality.

So once again, the problem is not what we perceive to be outside of us. The problem is that we have *chosen* to perceive it. Most of the time that choice is an unconscious one and thus we are not aware of it. Most of us would look out on some of the horrors that we perceive in the world and not realize that the horror we are seeing out there really comes from a decision to see it that way. The right-minded way of looking at what the world would call horror or catastrophe is to see it as a learning opportunity in which all people can join, because it stems from decisions that all people make to be a part of that situation. It is an opportunity that everyone — the seeming victim, the seeming victimizer, and oneself as the observer — is invited by the Holy Spirit to look at that situation and to see it differently.

Love's messengers are gently sent, and return with messages of love and gentleness.

This would be so regardless of what is perceived outside. Whether you are talking about a concentration camp in Nazi Germany, or someone who suffers as a result of an atomic bomb, or who is starving in Africa, or something that happens to a person in your immediate family, you can still look at what you are perceiving with gentleness and love.

The messengers of fear are harshly ordered to seek out guilt, and cherish every scrap of evil and of sin that they can find, losing none of them on pain of death, and laying them respectfully before their lord and master.

You will see toward the bottom of this page and the next just how graphic the Course is in describing what these messengers of fear bring back. Again, this has nothing to do with what is seen outside. The ego can find pain, guilt, horror, retribution, vengeance or abandonment in a situation that some people could see as happy and blissful. You could find fault and pain in anything if you are looking for it. Just as you can find love and gentleness in anything if you are looking for it.

Perception cannot obey two masters, each asking

for messages of different things in different languages.

Again, it is that all or nothing idea: you cannot obey two contradictory teachers or follow two contradictory thought systems. The reference here of course is to the Bible. While it is possible, through the process of dissociation, to split off mutually exclusive thoughts and retain both of them, this can only produce conflict, which is exactly what the ego wants. Remember that the ego was born out of conflict and needs it to sustain its existence. We shall return to this idea later.

What fear would feed upon, love overlooks. What fear demands, love cannot even see. The fierce attraction that guilt holds for fear is wholly absent from love's gentle perception. What love would look upon is meaningless to fear, and quite invisible.

Relationships in this world are the result of how the world is seen. And this depends on which emotion was called on to send its messengers to look upon it, and return with word of what they saw.

Again, we can substitute the word guilt for fear. A Course definition of a miracle is a shift in perception. Therefore, this is really a course to teach us how to perceive the world differently. Anything that we perceive in the world, all of which is some aspect of a relationship, is a result of how we see the world; which means how we see it within our minds or, even better, how we choose to see it.

In the following sentences the Course specifically addresses how the world is seen through the eyes of fear.

Fear's messengers are trained through terror, and they tremble when their master calls on them to serve him. For fear is merciless even to its friends. Its messengers steal guiltily away in hungry search of guilt, for they are kept cold and starving and made very vicious by their master, who allows them to feast only upon what they return to him. No little shred of guilt escapes their hungry eyes. And in their savage search for sin they pounce on any living thing they see, and carry it screaming to their master, to be devoured.

This is very, very powerful writing that certainly depicts the ugliness and purpose of the ego's world. This is a good place to comment on the Course's relationship to the world. While on the one hand the Course repeatedly teaches us that the world is illusory and therefore should not be taken seriously (Level One), on the other hand it teaches us how we experience this world that we have made (Level Two). Made to be an attack on God, this world is a place of terror, viciousness and savagery, as stated in the above passage. Before we can laugh away the insane world we made we first have to look at it — *as it is* — without fear and guilt. Passages such as this help us to do that.

Q: Is "master" being used here as synonymous with fear?

A: Yes. In a sense fear is the master that sends out these messengers; or you can substitute the word ego. It does not matter.

Q: So is it implying then that we are worshipping fear?

A: Right, which the ego of course does.

Send not these savage messengers into the world, to feast upon it and to prey upon reality. For they will bring you word of bones and skin and flesh. They have been taught to seek for the corruptible, and to return with gorges filled with things decayed and rotted. To them such things are beautiful, because they seem to allay their savage pangs of hunger. For they are frantic with pain of fear, and would avert the punishment of him who sends them forth by offering him what they hold dear.

It is very difficult to read lines like that and try to maintain that this is a course in sweetness and light, and that all one has to do is to call upon the Holy Spirit and all our problems will be taken from us. It is passages like this that point out the horror and the murderous intent of the ego system that is inside each of us. The problem is that most of this, if not all of it, is unconscious, and we are not aware of the murderous rage that is inside us, nor are we aware that we literally prey upon other people, psychologically if not physically.

In those sections on special relationships, especially in Chapters 16 and 24, we see more specifically the description of this preying on each other, trying to seize from others what we believe will give us salvation. In Chapter 24, when the Course specifically talks about the murderous intent of the ego, we can see how each of us could kill anyone, if not in deed then certainly in thought, as long as we believed that it meant salvation for us,

Q: Do you think that a lot of the violence that is being portrayed in movies today is a part of that unconscious aspect of the ego that we are not looking at?

A: I believe, not that the violence is any more than it was, but that its presence had been denied in other time periods. In the past a lot of people's emotions and feelings, both violent and sexual ones, for example, were really kept hidden and more repressed. Then a shift began in the late 50's and erupted in the 60's and 70's. There was a tremendous move away from that repression. The mood of the times was defiance of authority. Young people were rebelling against their universities, parents, ministers, priests, rabbis, and political leaders and representatives. What we were seeing then was the pouring out of all the violence that had been so repressed.

We live in a violent world. Many years ago I used to spend a great deal of time walking on the beach at Montauk Point, at the tip of Long Island. I remember once coming upon some seagulls who were pulling apart a fish, and feeling that it was the ugliest thing I had ever seen. It is that same kind of preying on other living things that we all do. I could not have found it so ugly if on some level it was not reminding me of some kind of deep ugliness in myself that I did not want to look at. When Gloria and I were at the Great Barrier Reef in Australia we saw how everything was preying on everything else, from the little micro-organisms all the way up the evolutionary ladder. It was a startling realization, not only about life on the reef but on the entire planet. The whole spectrum of physical life on the reef could be summarized in two basic characteristics: how organisms destroy other organisms, preying upon them to get food, and then how they attempt to ensure that they do not get preyed upon. The whole activity of physical life was attack and defense, whether we talk about a simple micro-organism or complex mammals. And this really is the world that we live in, that we have pushed down and prettied over.

The only difference between groups of people that we call primitive and ourselves is that they do not conceal this dynamic as much as we do. Freud was the first one to really pull aside the veil and show us what was really buried in our unconscious. Again, in the sections on specialness you can see that very graphically in terms of the kind of fantasies that we have. For example, we have a need to devour each other, incorporate each other, possess each other, rape each other, destroy each other. So it is not a pretty world that the ego has made. An important part of the Course's whole process is to show us exactly what this ugliness is inside of ourselves so we can then change our mind about it. At that point we can recognize that the whole thing is an illusion.

However, there is always a danger in working with this kind of process to cover this "dark" material over and then believe that we have undone it. We should never underestimate the power of denial to keep out of our awareness what we do not want to know or look at.

The following passage portrays the non-ego world of the Holy Spirit, elsewhere referred to as the happy dream.

The Holy Spirit has given you love's messengers to send instead of those you trained through fear. They are as eager to return to you what they hold dear as are the others. If you send them forth, they will see only the blameless and the beautiful, the gentle and the kind. They will be as careful to let no little act of charity, no tiny expression of forgiveness, no little breath of love escape their notice. And they will return with all the happy things they found, to share them lovingly with you.

Now we get the other side; the Holy Spirit's right-minded way of perceiving the world in contrast to the ego's wrong-minded way. The external world itself does not change; rather it is our mind that sees the world differently. The so-called vicious and savage are not condemned or blamed; rather they are seen as calling out for love. The "beautiful, gentle and kind" are the reflection of the love of Christ that is being called for. Seen in this way, the ego's world of hate and fear is transformed into the Holy Spirit's loving classroom in which we all learn together the happy lessons of forgiveness that will bring us back to God. One of the definitions of a special relationship is that it excludes. One of the definitions of a holy relationship is that it includes everyone. However, this does not mean that you literally invite everyone into your life; but it means that you do not exclude anybody on the basis of your own judgment based on fear, hatred or guilt.

Be not afraid of them. They offer you salvation.

This is a line that is repeated very often in the Course in different ways. Originally it was taken from the scriptural phrase "Be not afraid." Remember, the ego has taught us that we should be afraid. Recall again that the first line of this section states: "The attraction of guilt produces fear of love."

The ego has taught us that if we look with love at the world then the ego will be undone. And since we all identify with the ego, otherwise we would not be here, then we also identify with the ego's attraction to guilt and the ego's choice of the messengers of fear. So again, we are being told not to be afraid of the Holy Spirit's messengers of love and forgiveness, because salvation will come through them and not the messengers of hate.

Theirs are the messages of safety, for they see the world as kind.

They are kind because they do not see attack. Whether someone is acting in a way the world calls loving or hateful, the Holy Spirit's messengers bring back messages of love or calls for love.

Thus there is no threat and no danger. Knowing we are invulnerable, we are defenseless and thus totally kind. And it is this kindness we perceive in the world around us. This shift from the top line of the ego's fear in Chart A to the bottom line of the Holy Spirit's love and forgiveness is what constitutes the miracle.

Q: Take a situation where someone is telling me about his problems and I sense that this other person is in a state of despair. I begin to get afraid for that person and sense the despair. First of all, what you are saying is that I have sent out the messengers of fear, and therefore that is the only thing I am perceiving.

A: Right, which does not mean that you are responsible for the other person's despair or fear, but it does mean that you are responsible for your *perception* and *reaction* to it.

Q: Therefore, in that situation when I would begin to sense the despair and fear for this person, I would ask for help to have my mind healed; in a sense, to send out the messengers of love. What I would then see instead of despair and fear would be a call for help; their call and my call for help. At that instant the joining would take place.

A: Correct, you do not pray for the other person at that point, you pray for your perception to be healed. That is all you have to do. You also find this talked about in the beginning of "The Song of Prayer." It makes the point very clearly — i.e., you do not pray for others, you pray for yourself.

And all you need to do this is a little willingness.

If you send forth only the messengers the Holy Spirit gives you, wanting no messages but theirs, you will see fear no more.

That is exactly what we were just discussing. No matter what your eyes have seen or what the world would tell you is reality, you no longer see fear. The most extreme cases of this would be people who had been prisoners in death camps in the Second World War, and would have been able to go through that virtually without fear if they really were intent on sending out messengers of love. And so it is the extreme example, just as it was the extreme example of Jesus, that demonstrates and teaches us exactly what this principle is.

The world will be transformed before your sight, cleansed of all guilt and softly brushed with beauty.

And this, of course, would be the vision of the real world. To state it again, the world is transformed, not because anything external happens, but because we have chosen to see it through the eyes of the Holy Spirit. This next line is very important:

The world contains no fear that you laid not upon it. And none you cannot ask love's messengers to remove from it, and see it still.

Anytime that you perceive fear in the world it is

because you have put it there, simply because you could have made the choice to have seen a call for love instead. I am reminded of the lovely thought of St. John of the Cross: "Where there is no love, put love, and you will draw out love." Another way of saying the same thing is that if you look on a situation which is not loving, which is filled with fear, you can then make a different choice and choose the messengers of love. You "put love" there because you now perceive through the eyes of love, and then the situation is transformed in your perception.

Q: So when you say put love there, are you really saying it is your desire to see love beyond anything else?

A: I am saying choose love. That then becomes your prayer. You ask Jesus or the Holy Spirit for help: "Please help me see this situation the way You do." I think that is really the most meaningful prayer we could ever have. That really is what the Course means by saying that the only meaningful prayer is for forgiveness because we have everything else. It is a prayer to perceive a situation the way Jesus and the Holy Spirit perceive it, which means you do not deny what you see; you do not deny what is on the screen out here on the right-hand side of Chart A, but rather what you deny is your ego's interpretation of it.

The Holy Spirit has given you his messengers to send to your brother and return to you with what love sees. They have been given to replace the

hungry dogs of fear you sent instead. And they go forth to signify the end of fear.

Basically what this is saying is that we have a choice. Just as the last section of the text states, "Choose Once Again," we always have a choice of how we can look at a situation, which means the responsibility is always ours. Whenever we are tempted to see fear, hatred or murder, we can always choose to ask for help to perceive the situation in another way.

Occasionally I have been asked, "Is there any prayer in the Course that would be suitable as a grace before meals?" This next paragraph is the one that I mention. Also, from here to the end of the section there are specific references to the nature of communion, subtly correcting the traditional Catholic understanding of the Eucharist.

Love, too, would set a feast before you, on a table covered with a spotless cloth, set in a quiet garden where no sound but singing and a softly joyous whispering is ever heard. This is a feast that honors your holy relationship, and at which everyone is welcomed as an honored guest.

Love's feast is the substitute for the ego's feast — "the hungry dogs of fear." And the "table covered with a spotless cloth" is the table of forgiveness where there is no sin.

And in a holy instant grace is said by everyone together, as they join in gentleness before the table of communion. And I will join you there, as

long ago I promised and promise still. For in your new relationship am I made welcome. And where I am made welcome, there I am.

Communion, of course, means to join with each other, to come together, and one of the things that Jesus says in a few places in the Course is that he stands within the holy relationship. This of course does not mean that he is not present in the special relationship either. He says he is always present in our mind. But in the special relationship the guilt that we have chosen, which makes the relationship special, obscures him. It is like a veil that hides his presence. Choosing forgiveness instead of guilt removes the veil and we recognize him who was always there. So when Jesus says that he will join us there it does not mean that he has not been there before. He really means that he will join us there in our awareness of him. And what he waits on is our welcome. Elsewhere in the Course he says "that love waits on welcome." So, again, it does not mean that love is not present, but it means we will not be aware of it until we welcome it in.

And so this is the table of communion that he promised. Whatever it was that Jesus originally said or meant, in terms of the gospel account of the Last Supper, the blessing of the bread and the sharing of it certainly could not have been sharing his literal body since, as we will see later on, the body is nothing. So we cannot share something that has no value. It means he would share his love with all of us, which would be his presence when we choose to have him enter into the relationships in our lives. That is true communion, and that would have been the original inspiration of that moment recorded in the gospels.

I am made welcome in the state of grace, which means you have at last forgiven me. For I became the symbol of your sin, and so I had to die instead of you.

These sentences are very important in terms of explaining why Jesus says in a few places in the material that he needs us to forgive him. Within the ego system, perfect love (or perfect guiltlessness and innocence) is a sin. So the ego projected its own blasphemy onto Jesus who had to be killed to protect the ego system. Earlier in the text Jesus says, "to the ego the guiltless are guilty." And then still further down on that same page (224) he says, referring to himself: When the ego "was confronted by the real guiltlessness of God's Son it did attempt to kill him." There are many different ways of understanding this. Another way would be that each of us would feel condemned by ourselves for our sin of having abandoned God and having abandoned each other. And people who knew Jesus probably accused themselves of having abandoned him.

So then the ego can turn this around and Jesus would be seen as the one who abandoned us: He made all these promises and look how he let himself be captured, mocked, humiliated and finally killed. Therefore, the different ways of looking at Jesus would reflect different aspects of how the ego thinks.

To the ego sin means death, and so atonement is achieved through murder.

Certainly one of the key corrections the Course makes in reference to traditional Christianity is the whole idea of atonement through sacrifice, discussed in Chapter 3. The followers of Jesus saw in his death the atonement that God demanded through the sacrifice of His only Son. Within that clearly insane thought system, also expressed most powerfully in "The Laws of Chaos" in Chapter 23, God kills His Son who is innocent, so that he would be the atonement for the sins of the rest of the world. The statement "To the ego sin means death" is of course derived from the Pauline "The wages of sin is death," which the Course quotes earlier in this chapter.

Salvation is looked upon as a way by which the Son of God was killed instead of you.

This is a clear refutation of the whole concept of vicarious salvation, which states that through the suffering and death of Jesus we become saved, because Jesus was killed. The obvious insanity of this entire concept is exposed by the Course.

Yet, no one can die for anyone, and death does not atone for sin.

Death is a choice that we make, as we shall see under the third obstacle. And no one's death, including Jesus', can remove our responsibility for choosing sin and death. Death cannot and does not atone for sin. All that atones for sin is correcting the belief that sin demands punishment, i.e., forgiveness. "Atone" is a Course word that is synonymous with correction. In its traditional Judeo-Christian understanding, however, atonement connoted punishment and sacrifice. Certainly that is how the atonement, or the atoning death of Jesus was seen by the disciples. What atones for sin is simply realizing that it was an illusion, that it never happened in truth because the effect of sin is always separation, as it is also its source. The Course explains that we are not separate from each other because minds are joined, and it is that recognition that atones for, corrects, and undoes sin.

But you can live to show it is not real.

What is meant here is that sin is not real. On page 193 in the text Jesus says: "Teach not that I died in vain. Teach rather that I did not die by demonstrating that I live in you." We can show that sin is not real by demonstrating the principles by which Jesus lived, and the principles by which he still teaches us. Those principles are made real for us through forgiveness of each other. Now one of the Church's big mistakes, clearly implied in all of this, was that it made the body real. And so it took the gospel statements about Jesus' sharing his body with us and, whatever their historical accuracy, made them literal. Thus it became that Jesus gave up his *body* for us, suffered and died so that we would be saved. Then through the sacrifice of the Mass, which is how Catholics refer to it, that same sacrificial act is re-enacted over and over again. We then literally believe we are sharing in Jesus' body — the Catholic meaning of communion — which would be the last thing that he could ever have wanted us to do. Since Jesus' whole purpose in the crucifixion and resurrection was to show that he was not a body — in fact, that none of us is — it would make no sense for him to offer us a body he knew was nothing.

Furthermore, we find here the mistake of mixing up form and content that is constantly referred to in the Course. Rather than take the content of what Jesus was teaching — that he would always be with us to share his love with all of us, inviting us to share his love through our forgiving relationships — Christianity shifted his meaning by focusing on the body, using that as a way of excluding other bodies. That is how you can tell that the original message, if it did get through, got lost very, very quickly. The whole idea of being baptized and participating in the Eucharist was a very exclusive ritual that was only for those people who confessed the true faith. Anyone who did not partake in that was kept outside the Kingdom. Obviously that would be the very last thing Jesus would have taught, because his own words, even in the gospels, would show that he embraced all people.

As an extension of that same mistake of confusing form and content, we can look at the long history of Christianity's veneration of martyrs and its persecution of heretics, which we can trace back to the original misunderstanding of the crucifixion. Thus the ego is triumphant because everyone's guilt is reinforced either as a victim or a victimizer. It gets everyone, which is the ego's ultimate purpose, either through martyrdom or persecution; and the greatest martyr of all in the ego system would be Jesus. Moreover, the memory of Jesus is used to point the guilty finger at people who do not agree with what Christianity said Jesus taught. Thus he not only becomes a great martyr but also a great persecutor. From the point of view of many Jewish people, for example, it was literally Jesus who was murdering and persecuting them. A Jewish friend once asked me how I could become a Christian and believe in a Jesus who murdered all my people. Somehow in her mind this was all Jesus' doing. Therefore, you can see that to the Christians Jesus is the great martyr and to everyone else he is a great persecutor.

The body does appear to be the symbol of sin while you believe that it can get you what you want. While you believe that it can give you pleasure, you will also believe that it can bring you pain.

And in case you have skimmed these lines and missed them, they are repeated almost word for word in a couple of pages. The body *seems* to be the symbol of sin because sin is separation and the body is the embodiment of that thought. It is the body which was made to keep us separate from each other because bodies begin and have an ending, and the beginning and ending are separate from everyone else. Once we believe the body can get us what we want, whether we are talking about getting us what we want by murdering someone else, or getting what we want by being a source of pleasure, we are obviously making it real. If, however, we make the body real, then we are saying that sin and separation are real which means of course that God is not real. Therefore, believing the body to be an instrument or the source of pleasure is making it real. This reinforces the belief in sin, with the end result being the body will then bring us pain. Remember that sin leads to guilt, and guilt leads to the fear of punishment which is pain. So again, that is a very important line which we will return to in the next obstacle.

To think you could be safisfied and happy with so little (which is the body) **is to hurt yourself, and to limit the happiness that you would have calls upon pain to fill your meager store and make your life complete.**

So what the ego would have us do is identify with the body. Earlier the text contrasts the littleness of the ego with the magnitude of spirit. Here it is specifically talking about the littleness of the body, and the next obstacle talks about how the body is literally the nothingness of the ego. So when we choose to be satisfied with something that is so little, which is the body, we must hurt ourselves because we are excluding the only source of happiness in the world, which would be God. And the ego teaches that this littleness, this nothingness of the body, will make our life complete. That very important section on special relationships in Chapter 16, "The Choice for Completion," talks about the same thing. That is what specialness is all about: I can be complete by taking something from you and drawing it unto myself.

This is completion as the ego sees it. For guilt creeps in where happiness has been removed, and substitutes for it.

"Substitute" is one of the red flag words in the Course that always refers back to special relationships, which are a substitute for God. Where happiness is removed guilt creeps in and substitutes for it. If you think back to the gospel parable of "The Return of the Unclean Spirits," this is exactly the same idea juxtaposed. If you banish the evil spirits from your house and do not replace them with love, leaving your house empty, the evil spirits will return sevenfold. Seven is the Hebrew symbol for perfection, which means you get an infinite number of evil spirits which, of course, psychologically we now understand as being guilt. So when we remove happiness or love from our house, i.e., from our minds, then we leave a vacuum. And of course the banishing of love and happiness automatically brings guilt, which then becomes the substitute.

Communion is another kind of completion, which goes beyond guilt, because it goes beyond the body.

Again, this is a very subtle reference to the Roman Catholic understanding of communion. It has nothing to do with the body. Jesus did not give up his body for us; he does not share his body or blood with us. He shares his love, and that love is of the mind and embraces all people. That is the true meaning of communion, and that communion does complete us because out of the wholeness in my mind I now embrace the wholeness in you. I am not made complete by joining with your body because that is specialness. I am "made" complete by forgiving your body that had become a symbol of specialness (or separation). This heals my mind and restores to it the awareness of my own wholeness as Christ.

Q: Obviously there are a lot of people who work with the Course and are practicing Catholics. How can they look at the whole experience of the Eucharist differently?

A: They would have to look at it more the way that the Protestants have, in the sense that most Protestants saw the communion experience as being a symbolic one of joining with each other. It is the Catholics who teach that through the process of transubstantiation the body and blood of Jesus are *really present* in the Eucharist. The Protestants typically saw it as symbolic. So I think that if a Catholic were practicing the Course and following this thought system, that person would have to see the Eucharist as a symbol of joining with, not only Jesus, but all people. It would have to be an experience that united everyone whether they were Catholic or not, whether they were so-called sinners or not, since love would not depend on what the other person did or believed.

Q: Would you then have to have no investment in the Eucharist being something very special?

A: If you were going to work with the Course, yes. There is no way of justifying a belief that there is anything of the body or of the physical world that is holy or sacramental, or that has any value in and of itself. If you shift from the value inherent in the sacrament or holy object to the purpose that is given to the experience associated with it, then that of course is something else. The purpose then could always be one of joining and of love. But if you see that there is something inherently holy about an object or something in the world of form, or a person in the world of form, then that comes from a totally different system which would be incompatible with the Course. The Course always moves beyond the body and the form to the underlying content or meaning.

One final point about this section. The idea that the choice is ours in terms of what we are going to perceive in the world really contains the whole hope for peace in the world. As long as we continue to perceive enemies, whether in the Soviet Union, Central America or anywhere else, or perceive fear in any form, then there is no hope for bringing peace. The only way that peace can come into this world would be for individual people to change how they perceive this world and to accept responsibility for what they perceive.

There is a section later on in the text called "The Responsibility For Sight" that addresses this issue of accepting responsibility for what we perceive. I think this is the great contribution that the Course makes to the pursuit of world peace, and an important reason why the Course came at this point in time. The only hope of undoing the fear in the world is not by dismantling nuclear weapons, for example, because all that would happen is that more weapons would rise in their place. That could be a helpful place to begin, but the real shift is not outside here in the world, looking at the right-hand side of Chart A. The only place that the shift can occur is in the minds of people who make up this world of fear, over here in the left-hand side of the chart. This is something that we will come back to over and over again in these different sections. But again, I think this is the great contribution that the Course can make to the world at this particular time. The only peace that can come is when peoples' minds are healed.

PART II:
THE SECOND OBSTACLE

The Second Obstacle:
The Belief the Body is Valuable
for What It Offers

To summarize, the first obstacle to peace talked about our grievances and the ways we attack each other. Now in this obstacle we are talking about the value that the body has within the ego system, and specifically the value the body has for the ego in terms of pain. Remember that the ego's goal is to keep the body real, because if the body is real then the ego is real and God is not. So, the whole ego investment is seeing that pain is in the body. We will also find here material that bears on the way Christianity looked at Jesus — i.e., the belief in sacrifice, which is the source of pain.

We said that peace must first surmount the obstacle of your desire to get rid of it. Where the attraction of guilt holds sway, peace is not wanted. *TO LIMIT OR EXCLUDE SOME FROM FORGIVNESS. TO FIND THEM GUILTY.*
Again, that desire to get rid of peace is the desire to attack, which is what reinforces guilt. Moreover, it is one or the other; there is no in between. Peace and guilt, as we have seen with love and fear, are mutually exclusive states.

The second obstacle that peace must flow across, and closely related to the first, is the belief that the body is valuable for what it offers. For here is

71

the attraction of guilt made manifest in the body, and seen in it.

Most of the time we think that the body offers us pleasure, but the Course is teaching us that its gift is really pain. Pleasure and pain are opposite sides of the same coin because both serve to make the body real and thus reinforce our guilt.

VALUABLE

This is the value that you think peace would rob you of. This is what you believe that it would dispossess, and leave you homeless. And it is this for which you would deny a home to peace.

BODY-EGO
IDENTITY

If we choose peace then we are choosing against the body and guilt, and this obviously means we are choosing against pain. The ego teaches us that the body is our home, and so it is either we have the home of the ego or the home of peace. Again we cannot have both.

This "sacrifice" you feel to be too great to make, too much to ask of you. Is it a sacrifice, or a release?

EGO

The Course is telling us that the Holy Spirit would teach us that giving up the body and pain is a release. That is the "sacrifice" we feel we would have to give up if we chose peace, for the ego would have us believe that we would be losing something valuable. The major idea in this section is that the body is valuable for what it offers. If you are giving up something that is valuable then you are going to believe that you are sacrificing something.

72

What has the body really given you that justifies your strange belief that in it lies salvation? Do you not see that this is the belief in death? Here is the focus of the perception of atonement as murder. Here is the source of the idea that love is fear.

The gifts that the body offers us are just different ways of expressing its ultimate gift, which is death. If you think back to the story of Adam and Eve when they were punished by God for their sin against Him, God tells them that they will die. That is where St. Paul got the idea that the "wages of sin is death." So anything that we do, believe, seek after, or seek to avoid, is really making the body real. This means we are making death real because all bodies must eventually die.

If you remember "The Two Pictures" in Chapter 17, which deals specifically with special relationships, the ego's gifts, or picture, is put in an ornate frame, although the gift itself is a picture of death. Because we believe that the body is real, and we believe that salvation lies in the body, we must also believe that salvation lies in death, and that again is the strange belief that atonement for our sins comes through murder. And since we believe that we have to atone for the sin of turning against God and attacking Him, we then believe that God will punish us through murder. This murderous punishment by God of His children finds much support in the Bible. Finally, since God is Love we then make God and love fearful, and so we return again to the statement: "The attraction of guilt produces fear of love."

God

73

Q: Therefore, in a sense the Course is not asking you to make a sacrifice of the body, but to recognize that to let go of the body is no sacrifice. Is the Course advocating some kind of asceticism?

A: No, the Course does not point to or away from asceticism. That interpretation could only come from the confusion of the body with the mind, or the form with the content. What the Course is saying, which it actually makes clear in these sections and especially in the next one on "The Attraction of Pain," is that it is not the body that does anything. The body is not the source of sin; it is not the source of pleasure; it is not the source of pain; it is not the source of anything. And I think where people have made the mistake, and would make the kind of interpretation that you are talking about, is in seeing the Course pointing the guilty finger at the body. The body is not the problem.

If you refer back to Chart A, you can see that the problem is not what is in the body or the world, on the right-hand side of the chart, the problem is what is in the mind, on the left. It is the purpose that we have given the body that is our concern. So in essence what you give up, what you "sacrifice," is the decision to be fearful, guilty, unhappy and in pain. That is what the Course is saying: It is no sacrifice at all. But it is very easy to make the mistake of believing that we are to give up the body. Again, all that you give up is the ego's use of the body.

Q: But if you see the body, which all of us do, as a

source of pleasure, then it seems that that is what this particular section is addressing, i.e., we are stuck in the belief that in the body lies our salvation.

A: To really answer you, I have to go back to the idea of Level One and Level Two, and the confusion between them. On Level One the body is totally illusory and therefore it would be a mistake to give it any semblance of meaning, whether it is pleasurable or painful. But none of us is up to that level otherwise we would not be here. The more appropriate way of understanding this problem, Level Two, is that we do not deny our body's needs. We do not deny our body's pain. If we are hit over the head with a hammer, or if we do not have a coat and outside it is ten degrees below zero, we will be in pain. However, we do not have to make the body's pleasure or pain into a big deal. An important part of the Course's process is to help us move beyond the body as a focus of either salvation or damnation to the under lying thought system which gave rise to the body. That underlying thought system is separation, which is undone by joining with people in forgiveness.

The mistake, for example, that the Gnostics made — because they too recognized that the body was not made by God and that the world was an illusion — was that they skipped over all the intermediate steps, immediately jumping to the idea that to get involved with the body was sinful. All that does is make the body real. They confused Levels One and Two. The Course begins with the same basic metaphysics as did the Gnostics, but its whole process is a much more gentle and loving one, and actually it is much more authentic because it allows for the tremendous investment in the body that we all have.

So we do not disappear into the heart of God today; not even tomorrow. It takes a long, long time for us to change our mind from its tremendous investment in guilt and fear to the recognition that what we want can be achieved only by a step by step process of healing all of our relationships. But many people misunderstand this and confuse levels, and then move to the idea that since the body is an illusion one does not get involved with the body at all. But all that happens then is the denial of bodily impulses. It says in Chapter 2: "The body is merely part of your experience in the physical world. . . . However, it is almost impossible to deny its existence in this world." To shift our perception from the body as salvation to a perception that salvation is the healing of the mind — that is the Course's point.

The Holy Spirit's messengers are sent far beyond the body, calling the mind to join in holy communion and be at peace. Such is the message that I gave them for you.

The Holy Spirit moves beyond the body to the mind. That is where the problem is and that is where communion is; communion is not of the body, it is of the mind. And then Jesus makes it very clear that he did not give the message that he is quoted as having given in the New Testament.

It is only the messengers of fear that see the body, for they look for what can suffer. Is it a sacrifice to be removed from what can suffer? The Holy Spirit does not demand that you sacrifice the hope of the body's pleasure; it *has* no hope of pleasure.

Again, Jesus' basic teaching in the Course about the crucifixion is that he did not suffer. So he gave us the message to join in communion on the level of the mind. We are not to seek for anything in the world to give us pleasure. Much later in the text is a section called "Seek Not Outside Yourself," which asks us not to seek outside ourself for any idol, any special relationship that we believe can give us pleasure.

But neither can it bring you fear of pain.

Again, the body literally does nothing. It simply carries out the wishes of the mind. The ego sees the source of pleasure and pain in the body, but the only real pleasure comes in doing God's Will, and pain comes from denying it.

Q: Should you recognize that even if you are attracted to something outside yourself, it is not the thing itself that attracts you, it is just some value that you have given it in your mind?

A: Right, but do not deny the things in this world that give you pleasure; just do not make it into a big deal. Because if you deny it and do not allow yourself to enjoy the things in the world whether it is food, taking a walk, wearing certain clothing, listening to music or whatever, then you are making it real. The idea is just not to make a big deal out of it, and realize that real pleasure is coming from another place.

Pain is the only "sacrifice" the Holy Spirit asks, and this He *would* remove.

The only thing the Holy Spirit asks us to give up is pain, and pain comes whether you choose pleasure or pain as the world judges it.

— Peace is extended from you only to the eternal, and it reaches out from the eternal in you. It flows across all else.

Earlier in this chapter is a line that says, "Let then your dedication be to the eternal," and that is picked up in the next few pages too. The Course is asking us to let the peace that comes from the Holy Spirit, the eternal in us, extend through us to greet the eternal in someone else. It is the attraction of love for love that the text talked about in Chapter 12. It is the love of Christ in me calling out to the love of Christ in you.

The second obstacle is no more solid than the first. For you want neither to get rid of peace nor limit it. What are these obstacles that you would interpose between peace and its going forth but barriers you place between your will and its accomplishment?

Again, the barriers to our feeling peaceful have nothing to do with what is outside in the world.

They have only to do with a decision that we make; it is a barrier that we place between our will and its accomplishment. Our will is held in place for us by the Holy Spirit, and its accomplishment is the extension of it. So we have to remove the obstacles that would block this extension.

You want communion, not the feast of fear. You want salvation, not the pain of guilt. And you want your Father, not a little mound of clay, to be your home.

This is referring back to the previous section. That "little mound of clay" is the body. By the way, the second creation story in Genesis says how God made Adam from soil or clay. That is the body.

In your holy relationship is your Father's Son. He has not lost communion with Him, nor with himself. When you agreed to join your brother, you acknowledged this is so. This has no cost, but it has release from cost.

Over and over again the Course emphasizes that God's Will for us is not sacrifice. We are not giving up anything. Asceticism teaches giving up the pleasures of the body and the world. What is stated so clearly here is that this world has no pleasure; the body has no pleasure. It is a decision of how we see the world and the body that gives pleasure or pain. Therefore in our forgiveness of each other we remove the ego's veils that would keep hidden from us the recognition of the Christ in us.

You have paid very dearly for your illusions, and nothing you have paid for brought you peace.

What we have paid dearly for is our illusions of this world, the illusions which make the body real and which reinforce our belief in the reality of sin and guilt. This also has made real the sacrificial atonement that is the ego's plan to save us from our sins. All this has only brought us a continuation of pain and a lack of peace. The very salvation plan the ego has erected brings more pain, because it makes the body real. Its plan makes us resent God even more, because we believe He demands punishment for our sins against Him by demanding sacrifice of the body and the giving up of what we want. And this is exactly what the next line says:

Are you not glad that Heaven cannot be sacrificed, and sacrifice cannot be asked of you?

This is the true good news that the Course brings, that God does not demand sacrifice. We do not have to give up anything, we merely have to shift how we look at everything. Again, that is why Chart A is so important in order to understand how the Course suggests we look at the world. We do not try to change the world we just try to change our mind about it.

There is no obstacle that you can place before our union, for in your holy relationship I am there already. We will surmount all obstacles together, for we stand within the gates and not outside.

How easily the gates are opened from within, to let peace through to bless the tired world!

What Jesus is saying is that no matter what we do, no matter how much guilt we dump on each other through our special relationships, it cannot stop the fact that he is already there. This is reminiscent of the opening pages of the manual which describe how into this hopeless, dreary and closed learning situation God sends his teachers to bring a different vision and a different message.

Can it be difficult for us to walk past barriers together, when you have joined the limitless? The end of guilt is in your hands to give. Would you stop now to look for guilt in one another?

Now what Jesus is really calling for here is the end of projection. Rather than try to see sin and guilt in other people, we recognize it in ourselves and through joining with each other, letting Jesus take us by the hand, we together walk past all the barriers of guilt. And that is what changes a tired and despairing world into one that is filled with light and hope. Not because the world changes, but because our minds looking at the world have changed.

Once again we can see the important role the Course will have in bringing about true peace in this world. Peace is within and it is not without. Moreover, we cannot do this without joining with each other and joining with Jesus. He says in the workbook, and very clearly, that he is the one who saves the world through us. It does not seem very easy because we are still so attracted to our guilt. It *is* easy when we take his hand and ask his help to forgive those people we have condemned.

Let me be to you the symbol of the end of guilt, and look upon your brother as you would look upon me.

Here again Jesus is urging us to shift the perception of him that the world has had for two thousand years, because he became a symbol of our guilt as we saw in him God's punishment for our sins. Furthermore, we saw in him the exalting of sacrifice as the principle of atonement. Therefore none of us could look upon his suffering and dying body without feeling even guiltier. We would look from a perception of our own sinfulness, see this man who was totally sinless, and feel guilty because he suffered and died because we were bad. There is no way that that system could not bring about the reinforcement of the very guilt that Jesus came to teach us to let go of.

Forgive me all the sins you think the Son of God committed. And in the light of your forgiveness he will remember who he is, and forget what never was.

The emphasis here is that we should forgive Jesus all the things that we are really accusing ourselves of: sin, attack, murder and sacrifice which, once again, Jesus has become the symbol of. We basically accuse ourselves of the sins of judgment. And so we have projected that role onto him and he becomes the Lord of Judgment, judging the sheep and the goats, the wheat and the chaff; punishing the bad ones and rewarding the good ones. Except what is wrong is that deep within the hearts of everyone is the belief that we are the bad ones, we are the sinners. So no matter how we try to rationalize and theologize about it, there is a part, deep within us, that believes that the punishment Jesus will mete out must include us.

I ask for your forgiveness, for if you are guilty, so must I be.

If we persist in believing that we are guilty and that we are sinful, then we must project that onto Jesus and see him as attacking us. This does not mean that he is guilty in and of himself. It means we will perceive him as guilty, guilty of the sin of judgment and of sacrifice, i.e., exactly what we feel ourselves to be guilty of.

But if I surmounted guilt and overcame the world, you were with me.

Jesus showed that guilt is an illusion and is not justified, and he overcame the world of the body, sin and separation. He did it for all of us since minds are joined. He conclusively proved that the principle of the Atonement is true; the principle being that the separation is not real, guilt is not real, and that we are not separate. He lived out that principle perfectly. He says in the Course that the plan called for someone to set the Atonement into motion, and that is what Jesus did. Again, if he did this then we must be with him because minds are joined. The manual says that he was with us when he arose. It is the same idea.

Would you see in me the symbol of guilt or the end of guilt, remembering that what I signify to you you see within yourself?

So the whole image of Jesus that we have made, and that we have erected theologies on, has nothing whatsoever to do with him. It has only to do with our own guilt which we projected onto him. Remember, the ego's law is that guilt demands punishment, suffering and sacrifice, and so Jesus, from the ego's viewpoint, became someone who: 1) was punished by God, suffered and was sacrificed because of our sins; and 2) then in turn demands the same thing of us. Thus the Course urges us to see him as a symbol of the end of guilt, which means a symbol of pure forgiveness, to see him as the greatest manifestation of the Love of God the world has known.

From your holy relationship truth proclaims the truth, and love looks on itself. Salvation flows from deep within the home you offered to my Father and to me. And we are there together, in the quiet communion in which the Father and the Son are joined.

Because the truth in me looks on the truth in you, because the love in me calls for the love in you, and vice versa, there are no barriers that we put between us. And now we see the real meaning of communion as the Course understands it. It is recognizing the oneness of the Father and the Son. Jesus then becomes the symbol and bridge of the oneness of Heaven and the oneness of Christ that is in each of us. And that is the quiet communion in which the Father and the Son are joined, and that is what occurs in the relationship which is made holy. Moreover, that is what the Course means when it says that the temple of the Holy Spirit is in a relationship and not a body. It is the holy relationship that makes the Holy Spirit present to us, and that is what makes us aware of Jesus' presence in us. The temple of the Holy Spirit is in the mind that joins with someone who had formerly been seen as separate.

O come ye faithful to the holy union of the Father and the Son in you!

That is one of the rare exclamation points that you will find in the material. Again it is really a plea on Jesus' part that we join with each other and with him, which we cannot do if we persist in seeing him as a symbol of sacrifice and punishment.

And keep you not apart from what is offered you, in gratitude for giving peace its home in Heaven. Send forth to all the world the joyous message of the end of guilt, and all the world will answer.

What is offered you in gratitude is the love and joy of God. Once again we can see the next statement in the context of the situation we are in in this world. This is the very situation in which the Course came. The way that we become peacemakers is to give forth to the world this joyous message that we are not separate, and that we are all one regardless of what the world teaches, regardless of what bodies seem to tell us. If we send out that message then all the world will answer.

Naturally the faith on the part of the miracle worker or of the teacher of God is to see that answer to that call, even if it is not perceived by the body's eyes. This is not to be understood as saying that if a group of people change their minds then that will correspondingly effect a manifest change in the world. It will not happen that way. We have to realize the commitment that we have to fear and attack, punishment and death. It is so great that there will have to be, within the world of time, a period that will elapse between the time that the miracle is offered and the time that it is accepted.

But the Course promises us that when a miracle is offered it *is* accepted. Jesus holds that miracle until the time that people can let go of their guilt and receive what has already been given. If you go by the world's laws — that you must see the change in order to believe in it — then nothing will happen. In other words, you will then become part of the same insane system that you are trying to heal. All you have to do is change your mind, and trust that Jesus will take that joyous message of forgiveness and the end of guilt and extend it to the world. It will ring out, and those people with ears will hear and those with eyes will see. Those people who are still afraid will shield themselves from that light, but the light will nonetheless still be within them.

Think of your happiness as everyone offers you witness of the end of sin, and shows you that its power is gone forever.

Again, this is not necessarily something you experience on the level of the body. It is something that you will experience in your mind, and the peace within you will remain, regardless of what happens in the world around you. But your peace will then become a very powerful witness that at some point the world will recognize. The whole point of the Course is that people will grow to understand, practice, and increasingly live its message so that true happiness and peace will affect more and more people and eventually become commonplace.

Where can guilt be, when the belief in sin is gone? And where is death, when its great advocate is heard no more?

The belief in sin is the belief in being separate, which then automatically gives rise to guilt. The punishment for sin, which is what guilt demands, is death. So death as punishment will no longer be seen as real when the belief in it is no longer held.

Forgive me your illusions, and release me from punishment for what I have not done.

Just as the Course's version of the Lord's Prayer, at the end of Chapter 16, starts with "Forgive us our illusions, Father," Jesus is asking us that we forgive him the illusions of hatred, separation, sacrifice, suffering and murder that we have placed upon him. Psychologically speaking, there is a part of us that is always seeking to punish Jesus: First, by seeing him as being punished on the cross. Since "projection makes perception," we could not perceive Jesus as being punished on the cross had we not first wanted to have him be punished on the cross. Second, we indirectly believe we can punish Jesus by denying his teaching and example through our unforgiveness of others, ourselves and him, not to mention making him into a symbol of suffering, sacrifice and judgment.

I would think, however, that even people who do not experience a relationship with him have on some level been affected by him. It is very hard to grow up in the western world without being affected by the figure of Jesus, whether you are a Christian or a Jew, an atheist or a believer. It would be very difficult to avoid the issues raised by this man who has become the greatest and most powerful symbol of God in the western world. We can then see that what Jesus was doing through his crucifixion was re-enacting for the world the original "crucifixion" — the separation from God. Just as God's "sin" to the ego was the perfect Love of the Creator for the created, so too was Jesus' "sin" the perfect Love of Christ for Christ. Therefore, the egos of the world, bound by their own insane thought system, must continually attempt to destroy and murder the Love of Heaven in all its symbols and manifestations.

So for those who do not consciously relate to Jesus, I certainly would not recommend that they force him on themselves. But I think they should at least be open to the idea that there may be a part within themselves that they are not in touch with, that does have these kinds of unforgiving feelings.

So will you learn the freedom that I taught by teaching freedom to your brother, and so releasing me.

It is the same idea as "What you do to the least of these you do unto me," from the parable of "The Last Judgment" in Matthew 25. By releasing our brothers or sisters from the bondage of guilt that our projection placed them in, we are also releasing Jesus. Attacking other people reinforces our own guilt, which in turn reinforces our belief that we are undeserving of God's Love. Therefore the ego must keep Jesus' love away from us, thereby "imprisoning" him in terms of preventing his love, due to our unacceptance of it, from embracing us. On the other hand, by forgiving others, "teaching freedom to your brother," our guilt is undone which allows us to accept God's Love through Jesus. Thus is he released.

I am within your holy relationship, yet you would imprison me behind the obstacles you raise to freedom, and bar my way to you.

So that, to state it again, you do not have to consciously work on your relationship with Jesus. He will show up by himself when you release him from the prison of guilt in which you placed him.

And you do that by releasing the persons whom you have been attacking.

Yet it is not possible to keep away One Who is there already. And in Him it *is* possible that our communion, where we are joined already, will be the focus of the new perception that will bring light to all the world, contained in you.

The One Who is already there would be the Father who is talked about in the previous paragraph. Therefore it is in God that we are already joined with Jesus. Here is the word communion again; and in that communion, which is eternal, Jesus has already joined with us, joining us with God. All that is needed is that we remove the obstacle to the awareness of his presence.

It is this communion, this joining with Jesus through forgiveness, that becomes the focus of this new perception which is the true perception of the vision of Christ that will bring light to all the world. Once again, we can see this as a real call that we be instruments of this light to bring it to the world for this is the only way that peace will ever come. Peace cannot come by changing something on the level of the body. It cannot come by changing structures alone. It can only come by changing our minds, and in that way we can affect the minds of other people. But that light is not in the world as such, the light is in us, in our mind.

The Attraction of Pain

Let us move on now to the second section of the second obstacle, "The Attraction of Pain." Again, as I said at the beginning, the sub-sections in the first two obstacles, "The Attraction of Guilt," and "The Attraction of Pain," are both saying the same thing in different ways, as is the third obstacle, the attraction of death. We choose the experience of guilt, pain and death as they are ways of making the body real.

Your little part is but to give the Holy Spirit the whole idea of sacrifice. And to accept the peace He gives instead, without the limits that would hold its extension back, and so would limit your awareness of it.

Again, the whole idea is that we have to give over to the Holy Spirit our belief that sacrifice is salvation. Moreover, we believe that there is something meaningful and important in giving up the body, for that is the sacrifice that God demands as punishment. All we have to do is accept the peace that the Holy Spirit offers us. If we believe in the reality of the body then we are limited and love is limited, because the body in itself is a limit. Therefore, identifying ourselves only as a body is one of the key obstacles that prevents peace from extending from us into the world.

For what He gives must be extended if you

would have its limitless power, and use it for the Son of God's release. It is not this you would be rid of, and having it you cannot limit it.

The idea here is that the Holy Spirit is continually extending His peace, and all we have to do is get our ego selves out of the way. The specific way that we would express that would be through forgiveness; and that is the way the Son of God is released from his guilt.

If peace is homeless, so are you and so am I. And He Who is our home is homeless with us.

Because we are all one, what we do to each other we do to Jesus. And we make peace homeless by having guilt or sacrifice be our home. The second sentence means our Creator, because ideas leave not their source. If we are without a home, then our Creator, of whom we are an extension, is also homeless. Obviously, this is meant metaphorically because God cannot be homeless, although we may believe our attack on Him has rendered Him so.

Is this your wish? Would you forever be a wanderer in search of peace? Would you invest your hope of peace and happiness in what must fail?

This last phrase refers to some manifestation of the body. And again, what the Course is pointing to over and over again is the choice we make between the murder of the ego and the miracle of the Holy Spirit. Once we can see the choice clearly we can make a better choice. Without seeing clearly we cannot do that. That is why in the last sentence of Chapter 23 Jesus says: "Who with the Love of God upholding him could find the choice of miracles or murder hard to make?" The problem is that we are not aware of this, and so do not believe that the ego offers us murder, regardless of the form it takes.

Faith in the eternal is always justified, for the eternal is forever kind, infinite in its patience and wholly loving. It will accept you wholly, and give you peace. Yet it can unite only with what already is at peace in you, immortal as itself.

This is the theme of putting our faith in the eternal, in God and in God's Love. We cannot seek for peace outside of ourself, because there is nothing outside ourself. As the Course states, projection makes perception. If you are totally at peace within, all you will experience is peace without, regardless of the external situation. This is because, as some quantum physicists also tell us, there is no distinction between the inner and the outer: They are one and the same. Krishnamurti also emphasized this same point over and over again.

The body can bring you neither peace nor turmoil; neither joy nor pain. It is a means, and not an end. It has no purpose of itself, but only what is given to it. The body will seem to be whatever is the means for reaching the goal that you assign to it.

This is a very important statement. You could

not ask for a more important set of statements in
the Course in terms of what it is teaching. The
body does absolutely nothing. The body will
seem to be whatever is the means for reaching the
goal that you assigned to it. The section called
"Setting the Goal" in Chapter 17 says that we set
the goal, and then the means will fall in line with
that goal. The goal is either truth, peace, and joy,
or illusion, sacrifice, and pain. And the body will
simply do what the mind tells it to do. So once
again what we are talking about is going back to
the choice point which is in our mind (the left-
hand side of Chart A), where we choose how we
will use the body: either to be an instrument of
fear or an instrument of love. The choice again is
ours. It has nothing to do with the body or with
other people's bodies, on the right-hand side of
the chart.

This is also the key principle in back of the Bud-
dhist teaching of non-attachment; that you do not
detach from the things of the world as things, you
detach from your investment in the things. John
of the Cross actually taught the same concept,
i.e., the problem is not in the things of the world,
it is our attachment to the things of the world.
The great mystical and spiritual traditions of the
world were all basically teaching the same principle. Unfortunately the principles were not gener-
alized in the complete way that the Course does,
and that is why the mistakes happened in all
forms of religion, East and West. Again, the problem is not what we see of the world and the body
through our individual lenses, but rather our attachment to them. Our attachment should be to

the Holy Spirit's purpose, which is to see the body as an instrument of forgiveness, rather than the ego's attachment, which uses the body to separate, exclude and punish.

Q: If we find ourselves on a hot day in the summer feeling very uncomfortable because of the heat, we may think how did I get myself into this position? I surmise we are experiencing then the effects of a decision we made deep in the past. Even though we know it can be altered now, we do not make a connection that we made that decision. Is that correct?

A: The Course again, as we were saying earlier, would not suggest that you go back to that original decision. I think it would say that if on a hot day you are uncomfortable you should do whatever it takes to lessen the discomfort, such as change your clothes, take a shower, jump into a pool, drink something cold, and so on. The crucial idea would be to remember that what placed you into that mess of having a body that is sticky and uncomfortable is believing in separation, and all that follows from that. That is the problem you want to undo! You want to get back to the source of the problem, and the best way of undoing the belief in separation is to join with someone.

One of the major ways in which the Course would define joining is sharing a common goal; or, stated another way, not to see another's interest as separate from your own. So that would be the bottom line in terms of the practical implications of all of these principles. But it would not say that in the meantime you should not do something on the level of your body so you feel a little more comfortable. If anything, that would probably put you in a better frame of mind to join with and forgive someone. Just as if you are starving to death you are not going to think about undoing a grievance that you have towards someone. You think first of bringing some relief to your hungry body. Furthermore, there is nothing in the Course to suggest that you should not do that. The Course repeatedly says that it is simple. You do not put your body through discomfort or torture in order to realize you are not your body. The idea is to be practical, gentle and merciful with oneself, facilitating what is really important, which is the undoing of our guilt towards each other by asking the Holy Spirit's help to forgive.

Peace and guilt are both conditions of the mind, to be attained. And these conditions are the home of the emotion that calls them forth, and therefore is compatible with them.

Now this is the exact thing we talked about in the previous obstacle regarding the messengers of love and fear. That "peace and guilt are conditions of the mind," and they must "be attained," means that they are learned. This is another way of saying that this is a course in learning. We taught ourselves the ego system, which is guilt; God did not give it to us. Therefore we now have to learn another system which is really a process of unlearning. We unlearn the guilt of the ego and then naturally the Holy Spirit's truth and love will emerge in us. We do not have to worry about learning His lessons of love. What we have to do is learn His lessons of undoing the guilt that the ego put there. We therefore come back to that choice point in our mind, on the left-hand side of Chart A, when we chose to learn guilt, and now we can choose again and learn peace.

But think you which it is that is compatible with you. Here is your choice, and it *is* free.

The question that we should ponder on, as is stated earlier in the text, is: "Who is the you who are living in this world?" If we identify with a "you" that is weak, puny, and inadequate, ridden with guilt and sin, then obviously we are choosing an emotion of fear, and that is what we will choose to be compatible with. If we can shift our identification and remember that we are as God created us — we are not bodies but are free, as the workbook says — then we realize that our true Self is holy, innocent and love. It is that Self that calls forth witnesses in the world that will reinforce our choice.

But all that lies in it will come with it, and what you think you are can never be apart from it.

So that once we choose between identifying with the weakness of the ego or the strength of Christ, an entire thought system is set into motion. And the problem is never what is within that thought system, i.e., the messages brought back by fear's messengers. The problem always is in the decision we made in our mind to choose an ego thought system. That is why the Course teaches that analysis is of the ego. The ego analyzes, the Holy Spirit accepts. The ego analyzes the system it made up because that is what roots us in it; the Holy Spirit simply looks past the ego's illusions and accepts the truth as God created it.

The body is the great seeming betrayer of faith. In it lies disillusionment and the seeds of faithlessness, but only if you ask of it what it cannot give.

It *seems* to be the body that disillusions us, is faithless and is a betrayer, that hurts and harms and that is hurt and harmed; but that is only because we choose to have the body be that for us. It seems that the body is what betrays us and is the locus of sin; however, it is not the body that "betrays," but the mind that chose that the body have this role. Once again, this does not mean that we deny our body. Remember that important difference between Level One and Level Two. On Level One the body is a symbol of sin because that is how we have made and used it. But that does not mean that we attack the body or that we deny our body. It does not mean that we deny our body's pleasures or pains. We but simply begin the process of asking the Holy Spirit's help in reinterpreting what we have made, and have Him help us in gently correcting our mind about it. This occurs on what I have called Level Two. And the way of proceeding is not to focus on the silly things that we do with our body, believe about our body, or seek for with our body, but to correct the ways that we use our body to attack each other. That is much more to the point because that is where our guilt is most firmly rooted.

Can your mistake be reasonable grounds for depression and disillusionment, and for retaliative attack on what you think has failed you?

The mistake Jesus is referring to here is the mistake of choosing the body instead of the Christ in us. He furthermore urges us not to use that mistake as grounds for reinforcing our belief that the world has victimized us, or that we have victimized the world.

Use not your error as the justification for your faithlessness. You have not sinned, but you have been mistaken in what is faithful. And the correction of your mistake will give you grounds for faith.

In the beginning of this chapter there is a section called "Healing and Faith," which talks about faith and how you put your faith in the Christ in yourself, i.e., in your strength as Christ and not in the weakness of the ego. The idea that we have not sinned but have been mistaken is found in the early sections in this chapter which deal with sin and error. A lot of discussion also focuses on how the Son of God believes all kinds of terrible things but he cannot sin; for example: "The Son of God can be mistaken. . . . But he *cannot* sin."

And we have been mistaken by what we call

faith. We have believed that it is the body that is a symbol of faith or faithlessness, and we then judge accordingly. For example, we believe certain people are faithful and can be trusted and others cannot be trusted. All such decisions are made in terms of the body and they end up excluding certain people. All Sons of God are symbols of faith if we can see in them the light of Christ, rather than the darkness of the ego. The correcting of this mistake with the help of the Holy Spirit, the shifting of our perception of someone else's body, will show us that we can indeed trust the light of Christ that shines in them and, of course, that shines in us as well.

Q: I am not sure how practical it is to trust all people, especially those we have had sad experiences with.

A: It is a principle that we aspire to, and that is the idea. It is a principle that we hold up as an ideal so that whenever we are tempted to forget, which is all the time, we can then go back and say I know there is another way of looking at this person. Even if at the moment you scream like a wild person and are having a massive ego attack, on some level you know this is not justified. When the Course says, "I trust my brothers, who are one with me," or asks us to trust that our brother will do his part, it does not mean that you trust his ego or anyone else's. You can, without anger, be aware of how this person's ego will not be trustworthy, will fail to keep appointments, or will fail to do things that he or she says would be done. It does not mean that. It means that you look at that situation without judgment and without anger.

Here is a reiteration of that same idea that we saw just before:

It is impossible to seek for pleasure through the body and not find pain.

In case we missed it the first time, Jesus is giving us a second shot at it. If we seek to make the body real by seeing it as an object of pleasure, we are inviting pain because we are making the body real. Now it also means that on an experiential level if we become dependent on something or someone in this world as a source of pleasure, and that person or that object is absent, we will feel deprived of that pleasure and that deprivation would be experienced as pain.

Again, the Course does not say we should ascetically strip ourself from all people and things. It is simply reminding us that as we are finding pleasure in the world, we should recall that the body is really not where it is at. And so at the same time that we are enjoying something or someone's company, we also recognize that that is not the Kingdom of Heaven. So, for example, if something happens and a certain person or object is not there, we are not devastated by their absence. But the ego would teach us that they are absent because God is punishing us. So it is the ego's god who is teaching us that we should not be attached to this person and that again makes God into someone who is punitive and brutal, and thus makes Him as insane as we are. The right-minded way of looking at it is that this is a lesson for us to learn. We can still be at peace even if this person or situation is not present.

It is essential that this relationship be understood (between the body and pleasure and pain), **for it is one the ego sees as proof of sin. It is not really punitive at all. It is but the inevitable result of equating yourself with the body, which is the invitation to pain. For it invites fear to enter and become your purpose. The attraction of guilt *must* enter with it, and whatever fear directs the body to do is therefore painful. It will share the pain of all illusions, and the illusion of pleasure will be the same as pain.**

Here is a very clear explanation of how the ego will interpret pain as punishment for our sin. For example, I wanted something, I lusted after this person, and now I am being punished for it. It was a sinful thing and now it is being taken from me and this is God's punishment. But that is not where the pain is coming from. The pain is coming from a decision to make the ego real and God not real. And that decision automatically means we are attacking God, we are making our guilt and fear real, and the result in our mind will be the fear that God will punish us. That is what seems to happen and that is the meaning of the line: "It invites fear to enter and become your purpose."

The reason then for equating yourself with the body and seeking pleasure in the body is to choose to have fear come. It is the idea that "The attraction of guilt produces fear of love." The attraction of guilt must enter with fear because guilt comes when we make sin, separation and the body real. And therefore whatever happens after that is going to be painful. In other words, all illusions, even the pleasurable ones, end up as painful because they are illusions, and illusions have their birthplace in sin, and sin always leads to fear. Remember that the purpose of the ego is always to keep focused on the reality of the body.

Is not this inevitable? Under fear's orders the body will pursue guilt, serving its master whose attraction to guilt maintains the whole illusion of its existence. This, then, is the attraction of pain.

Another way of saying what these obstacles have been teaching is that the fear of the ego orders the body to be guilty. It does that by having us make pain something that we have to avoid, or pleasure something that we have to attain. Both alternatives make the body real to us. Thus the attraction of guilt keeps the body real, which keeps sin real, which is the whole illusion of its existence. So we come to a very vicious circle. We begin with sin which makes us guilty, and then we continue to be attracted to guilt and, by choosing guilt, we maintain the illusion of sin. And that is what pain does. Pain proves the body is real and then everything else of the ego's thought system becomes real as well.

Ruled by this perception the body becomes the

servant of pain, seeking it dutifully and obeying the idea that pain is pleasure.

The pain it is talking about here would not necessarily be the pain of sickness. It is talking about the pain that masquerades as pleasure. Anything that we invest in, in terms of the body being pleasurable, must bring pain because it keeps the ego system going.

It is this idea that underlies all of the ego's heavy investment in the body. And it is this insane relationship that it keeps hidden, and yet feeds upon. To you it teaches that the body's pleasure is happiness. Yet to itself it whispers, "It is death."

What is being described here again is that crazy idea that we all subscribe to that the world and the bodies in the world give us pleasure. Again, this is not to be interpreted as meaning we should not do things that give us pleasure. It means that we should not make them into a big deal, because that falls into the ego's trap of heavily investing in the body. Before we can be without all investment in the body we obviously must begin by decreasing that investment. This is not a course in asceticism. It is a course only in the gradual, loving and gentle release from guilt.

Why should the body be anything to you? Certainly what it is made of is not precious. (I believe over 90% of the body is water.) **And just as certainly it has no feeling. It transmits to you the feelings that you want.**

We believe the body feels. One of the big illusions that we all operate on is that the body feels pain because that is what our experience is. And we are not aware that the body simply carried out what our mind told it to do. We have made sickness real. We have made real certain things that occur to our bodies, and because of our belief in them, the body becomes real to us.

I remember Bill Thetford telling of an experiment he did when he was in college. He hypnotized a college student and told her that he was going to touch her arm with a red hot needle. Instead he touched her with a needle at room temperature. The student still developed a blister because her mind was programmed to believe that she would experience heat and pain when Bill touched her. Objectively he touched her with nothing that could have caused a blister according to physical laws, but because she believed the needle was hot her body acted accordingly. This example clearly illustrates the power of our minds. However, the ego's plan calls for the sudden repression or denial of the choice that it made, as emphasized in Lesson 136 in the workbook, "Sickness is a defense against the truth." So now we believe that the body is causing us pain, and forget that our mind originally told the body that it should feel pain. Remember that the body is totally neutral and simply carries out what the mind orders.

Like any communication medium the body receives and sends the messages that it is given. It has no feeling for them. All of the feeling with

which they are invested is given by the sender and the receiver.

They are one and the same, sender and receiver. Our ego mind sends the message, and our brain receives and interprets it, and transmits instructions to our body. It is the same idea that we send out messengers of fear and they bring us back fearful messages.

The ego and the Holy Spirit both recognize this, and both also recognize that here the sender and receiver are the same. The Holy Spirit tells you this with joy. The ego hides it, for it would keep you unaware of it.

Both the ego and the Holy Spirit follow the same process — sending out messengers to bring back the desired messages. The difference of course is their starting point: fear or love. The Holy Spirit reminds us that the messages are only in our mind. The ego teaches us that the messages that are brought back are from this world, thus splitting off the cause from the effects, splitting off the mind from the body.

Who would send messages of hatred and attack if he but understood he sends them to himself? Who would accuse, make guilty and condemn himself?

If we really knew and understood that by attacking other people we are attacking ourselves; if we really knew that by going after the pleasures of the world we really bring pain to ourselves,

none of us would do it. The problem is that we
have split off cause and effect and reversed it, as
those later sections in the Course state. We are not
aware that we are really receiving the message
that we sent out. The ego teaches us that the message comes from the right side of Chart A, where
the world is, without our realizing that the message really has come from the guilt in our mind,
on the left side. This is a very important theme in
the Course.

**The ego's messages are always sent away from
you, in the belief that for your message of attack
and guilt will someone other than yourself suffer. And even if you suffer, yet someone else will
suffer more.**

Now this is nothing more than our old friend
projection. We send our messages of guilt away
from us and we dump them on to other people in
the hope that they will suffer. Even if we have to
suffer, we yet believe that someone else will suffer
more. This is the ego's principle that "ideas *leave*
their source." The ego teaches us that the idea in
our mind *can* leave its source and go to someone
else. So the guilt in our mind can now travel to
someone else whom we have attacked as the enemy; then that person becomes the one who suffers and we are off the hook. And we believe that
we do not receive back the message that we sent.

The great deceiver (who is often referred to as the
devil, and obviously here as the ego) **recognizes
that this is not so, but as the "enemy" of peace, it**

urges you to send out all your messages of hate and free yourself. And to convince you this is possible, it bids the body search for pain in attack upon another, calling it pleasure and offering it to you as freedom *from* attack.

The ego knows exactly what it is doing. The ego wants us to attack other people because that is what reinforces our own guilt. Now, this dynamic works whether we are involved with others in the pursuit of pleasure — making their body and our body real which, because we are identifying the body as real, really constitutes an attack on them — or we are projecting our guilt on to other people and attacking them directly. Remember, pleasure and pain are really one and the same thing. So this is really talking about projection and the ego's belief that by sending the message of guilt out and projecting onto someone else we are free of it. The Holy Spirit tells us with joy that this is the source of all of our pain, and because it is in our mind we can change our mind about it. The reason I am upset is not because of what you have done, or even because of what my body has done; the reason I am upset is because of a decision I made in my mind, and because I made it I can now change my mind about it.

Hear not its madness, and believe not the impossible is true. Forget not that the ego has dedicated the body to the goal of sin, and places in it all its faith that this can be accomplished.

In the section called "The Incredible Belief," the text says do not believe the incredible. And the incredible or the impossible is that the ego is real. Remember that the Course is asking us always to keep in mind that the ego uses the body to reinforce separation and sin.

Its sad disciples chant the body's praise continually, in solemn celebration of the ego's rule. Not one but must believe that yielding to the attraction of guilt is the escape from pain. Not one but must regard the body as himself, without which he would die, and yet within which is his death equally inevitable.

We all believe the way we feel better is to project our stuff onto other people, either in the form of attacking them and bringing them pain, or projecting onto the body and believing that the body is a source of pleasure. Now this is the great paradox of the ego system, which does not let us realize that it *is* a paradox. Anyone who is a disciple of the ego must identify with the body; and we believe without the body we would die and yet within the body we must also die. So that is the strange reasoning that no one in this world really looks at. We are so invested in the body because that is what will keep us alive, and yet the body must inevitably die. People like Freud, for example, were so pessimistic because they recognized that from the moment we are born we are progressing steadily and inexorably towards our death, from which there is no way out. Moreover, within the ego system there is no way out.

It is not given to the ego's disciples to realize that they have dedicated themselves to death.

Now what we are seeing here is a gradual movement away from what has been talked about to glimpses of the third obstacle, which is death's attraction. We do not realize that our belief in the body as a source of pleasure or pain, and our belief in attacking other people — which are the first two obstacles — are really an expression of the deeper dedication to death.

Freedom is offered them but they have not accepted it, and what is offered must also be received, to be truly given.

We are not aware that freedom is really offered us from all the suffering of the world by shifting from the right-hand side of Chart A, the world of the body, to the left-hand side, our mind. But we have not accepted it; and we have not accepted it because we have not offered it. If we really want to have peace, then we must teach peace to learn it, as it says in the lessons of the Holy Spirit in Chapter 6. If we really want to receive peace then we must offer it. We can become instruments of peace in the world only by having peace begin within ourselves, as the Unity song states: "Let there be peace on earth and let it begin with me." Peace and freedom must begin within us, and as we extend them to the people in our immediate world through the removal of the obstructions of peace, the Holy Spirit extends that peace and freedom to the whole world.

For the Holy Spirit, too, is a communication medium, receiving from the Father and offering His

messages unto the Son. Like the ego, the Holy Spirit is both the sender and the receiver. For what is sent through Him returns to Him, seeking itself along the way, and finding what it seeks.

The Holy Spirit was sent by God into our deluded mind to bring His Love, so that we could hear that message and give it to the world. By the way, the most quoted biblical statement in the Course is "Seek and ye shall find," and you will notice that seeking and finding reference all the way through. The Holy Spirit is the presence of love in our mind and He is always sending out messengers of love that bring back messages of love. Again quoting John of the Cross, "Where there is no love, put love, and you will draw out love." That is the whole idea; we put love out into the world and we receive it back. Because there is no world outside of our minds we are really just giving the message to ourselves, and *that* is the purpose of the body. The mind gives the body the message of love so that we see the body as an instrument of communication rather than of separation, and that returns love's message to our mind.

So does the ego find the death *it* seeks, returning it to you.

The ego sends out a message of fear which ultimately is a message of death, and that is what it perceives in the world.

Q: How would you address the issue of people

who are not aware of ego dynamics and are continually seeking for what they think will bring them pleasure or happiness in the world? Then feeling once they have accomplished whatever they set out to do, that it did not bring them the happiness they had fantasized it would, and they have this deep aching feeling, a hole within. How would you approach people like that? What advice would you give them?

A: You mean clinically in a sense of how you would advise someone?

Q: Clinically, or people who are not aware of the Course and are not interested in a spiritual path, but are continually experiencing this feeling that they are going after something for pleasure and always experiencing that it is not quite bringing them what they think it is going to bring them.

A: I think the way that you approach that depends on the person. If people are not ready to hear this message at all, which I think would include most people in the world, what you can help them realize is that a lot of what they are seeking after is an escape from some pain that they do not want to deal with in themselves. For example, maybe they are really very dissatisfied with their job, their spouse or their families; perhaps there is some kind of grievance that they are holding; if they can become aware that they are using the external seeking as a way of camouflaging the deeper pain, becoming aware of that connection could be the beginning of a breakthrough. And I think that it is possible to work with people that way even if they do not want to buy this whole thought system, provided they can accept the recognition that their way is not working.

However, if you do not sense that recognition, then very often you cannot really help them using Course principles. Whatever the relationship is, I think you can at least begin to have them step away from what is outside of them and to look at what is within. There may be a deep pain in their life for many, many years that they have just avoided, or a sense of hopelessness or emptiness that they keep trying to fill up. From a clinical point of view, you must at least start where people are at. I would not say "do not go skiing any more," "stop drinking," or "stop this or that," because then people would experience it as a sacrifice. In a sense I would try to discourage them from putting all their eggs in that basket and look at what they are really running away from.

Q: How about people who realize that there really is nothing satisfying in this world but try to fill up that void with what they would consider exciting? Existentially they feel this loneliness or this deep emptiness, and yet they still try to fill it up continually with whatever, partying or things.

A: Again I think it is the same thing. If I were involved with such a person I would try to wait until I sensed there was some kind of signal that he or she was not satisfied and was ready to consider another approach. Just as in Bill's famous "There must be another way" speech, you have to wait until a person is ready. Very often you have to wait until the person almost hits rock bottom and realizes that nothing has worked. But you have to wait for an opening.

Q: Would that require that the people themselves have some introspection, have some honesty about themselves?

A: Yes, I think it does presume that. If they do not have some introspection and they get more and more despairing, then the only out might be suicide. When, as the Course implies at the beginning of Chapter 15, a person believes that the ego's is the only voice, and it is a voice of death and despair and there is no way out, then suicide becomes the answer. That line in the text, "There is a risk in thinking death is peace," is relevant here. There is very little we can do for someone who is not willing to recognize that there is something else. I think that is the ultimate step in the ego's plan; you move from the attraction of guilt, to the attraction of pain, to the attraction of death, which is the next obstacle. And death then becomes attractive. That is the ultimate proof that the ego is right.

Q: Rollo May wrote about a patient that he had who was going to commit suicide, and he did nothing overtly to stop the suicide. How would the Course look at that?

A: That is a difficult thing to comment on, without really knowing Rollo May or that patient. It certainly sounds, the way the story is usually told, that it was a distortion of this teaching from a Course perspective. I think it would be important that therapists not have an ego investment in the patient staying alive, because otherwise they become a victim of a patient's choices. But at the same time a therapist must recognize that the patient's choice for suicide is coming from a profound sense of separation, hopelessness and guilt. That is what you want to change. I think that there would be a way of doing that without: 1) trying to physically stop the person from suicide, which is impossible since there is no way you can do that; and 2) the other extreme of turning one's back and saying, "Well, it is your choice."

The idea is to recognize where the suicide is coming from and really try to get at its source, which is to help people have some idea that they are loved and that there is hope. But if people are closed and literally hell bent on suicide there is nothing you can do to stop them, unless you are willing to spend twenty-four hours a day with them, which obviously is not possible. I think that it could be a distortion of Course principles to say, "It is a person's choice and there is nothing I can do; it is his or her responsibility and so that is it." And wash your hands of the whole thing. That would not be loving or an expression of love. Asking the Holy Spirit for help would be the best way all around.

PART III:
THE THIRD OBSTACLE

The Third Obstacle:
The Attraction of Death (beg.)

The attraction of death is the deepest of the first three obstacles, and certainly within the ego system is the most powerful witness to the reality of the ego: If death is real then the body is real, which obviously means that the ego must be real. What seems to be the fear of death to most of us is just a camouflage that hides the fact that the ego is secretly attracted to death for the reasons that we just talked about. That is what the basic gist of this section is, and it brings up a couple of very important points which we will go into as we go through this.

To you and your brother, in whose special relationship the Holy Spirit entered, it is given to release and be released from the dedication to death. For it was offered you, and you accepted.

Once again, when we are in a special relationship fraught with illusions of love or feelings of pain and hatred, it does not seem as if that relationship is really dedicated to death. But if we are dedicated to hurting another person or ourselves then ultimately that must lead to death, since attack and death are part of the same thought system.

Now what is offered to us is the release from death. This immediately recalls the section, "The Two Pictures," in Chapter 17 which talks about

119

the ego's picture that is its gift of death, concealed by the allurements of the special relationship. It is this "gift" from which we need release, and this release comes through forgiveness.

Yet you must learn still more about this strange devotion, for it contains the third obstacle that peace must flow across. No one can die unless he chooses death. *CHOOSES THE EGO THOUGHT SYSTEM*

There is a very striking parallel to this in workbook lesson 152, "The power of decision is my own," which says: "And no one dies without his own consent." It is the exact same idea here. Certainly this is not our experience in the world, where it seems that death is something that comes to us because we are not aware of the choice we have made, having relegated it to the unconscious realm. Workbook lesson 136, "Sickness is a defense against the truth," states:

In that second, even less, in which the choice is made, you recognize exactly what you would attempt to do, and then proceed to think that it is done. . . . All this cannot be done unconsciously. But afterwards, your plan requires that you must forget you made it, so it seems to be external to your own intent; a happening beyond your state of mind, an outcome with a real effect on you, instead of one effected by yourself.

Most people in the world look at death as if something unasked for happens to their body: for example, one accidentally walks in front of a car, or boards a plane which crashes, etc. Therefore it does not seem that we have chosen all these experiences, and in a religious context people believe that God calls them back to Him. All this fits the ego's purpose very well by reversing cause and effect. It seems as if we are the victims of the world and the body, and thereby we never realize that the real problem lies in the choice our minds make; and without realizing it is in our minds we cannot change it.

What seems to be the fear of death is really its attraction. Guilt, too, is feared and fearful. Yet it could have no hold at all except on those who are attracted to it and seek it out. And so it is with death.

This is the same idea that we already considered in the previous obstacles: Guilt, pain and death are choices that we make, and none of these would have any hold on us if our egos were not attracted to them.

Made by the ego, its dark shadow falls across all living things, because the ego is the "enemy" of life.

As I mentioned before, one of the reasons Freud was pessimistic, not only in his personal life but certainly in his theory, was his understanding that from the moment that we are born we proceed to die. All of what we call life he saw as nothing more than an inevitable progression to death. That is why later in his life he talked about a death instinct (*thanatos*) which became the opposite force to the life instinct (*eros* or the *libido*). And that is what this is referring to in terms of the dark shadow. From the moment that we are born we live with the spectre of death over us. "The Substitute Reality," the beginning section in Chapter 18, and "The Two Worlds," the final section in that chapter, talk about the dark shadow that guilt casts upon the world; and of course the problem is that we have made the shadow real.

And yet a shadow cannot kill. *A PERCEPTION*

The word shadow can be understood as being the body, and when we come to the next section, "The Incorruptible Body," we will talk a great deal about this. The shadow of guilt in this world is the body, and it is the body that we believe dies, or the body that we believe kills another body.

What is a shadow to the living? They but walk past and it is gone.

When one's mind is fully awake, then one is truly alive and looks right past the flimsy shadows of the ego — guilt and the body. Here we see again the allusion to Plato's cave, which discusses the shadows that are cast upon the interior of the cave wall, and how the prisoners make those shadows out to be reality. It is the "living," the prisoner who turns around, walks towards the sun, the source of the light, who awakens to the truth and realizes that the shadows were nothing more than shadows and therefore not real.

But what of those whose dedication is not to live; the black-draped "sinners," the ego's mournful chorus, plodding so heavily away from life,

dragging their chains and marching in the slow procession that honors their grim master, lord of death?

This would include all of us who live in this world, believing that it is real. Even those of us who believe we are happy because our security needs are taken care of, still are not aware that we are part of the mournful chorus continually singing a litany to the lord of death.

Touch any one of them with the gentle hands of forgiveness, and watch the chains fall away, along with yours.

This is one of the Course's key ideas and a preview of the last section in this chapter, "The Lifting of the Veil." It is through forgiveness and the holy relationship that we pass through the third and fourth obstacles.

See him throw aside the black robe he was wearing to his funeral, and hear him laugh at death. The sentence sin would lay upon him he can escape through your forgiveness. This is no arrogance. It is the Will of God.

To the ego this would seem to be arrogance, but that is but the false humility of the ego. In the eyes of the world it does seem arrogant to be told that we have the power to forgive sins, which Christianity said belonged only to God or Jesus, while the Catholic Church taught that that power could be mediated through specially designated people — its priests. The Course's view obviously is quite different. God cannot forgive sins because

He does not know of them — as the workbook says: "God does not forgive because He has never condemned" — but because we do believe in sins through the power of our minds, that same power can correct our distorted perception through the help of the Holy Spirit.

What is impossible to you who chose His Will as yours? What is death to you? Your dedication is not to death, nor to its master. When you accepted the Holy Spirit's purpose in place of the ego's you renounced death, exchanging it for life.

Again, this is assuming that we have already chosen to forgive our special relationships rather than to continue them. The decision to look kindly at somebody whom we have attacked, the decision to look beyond the sins we project onto another person, is nothing less than a decision to choose life instead of death.

We know that an idea leaves not its source. And death is the result of the thought we call the ego, as surely as life is the result of the Thought of God.

This introduces a very important theme, one of the most crucial teachings of the Course: "Ideas leave not their source." I would like to digress to discuss this principle, and then illustrate it with a workbook lesson that talks about this very specifically in terms of death, after which I will return to this third obstacle.

"Ideas leave not their source."

Let us first consider "ideas leave not their source" in terms of Heaven and the ego. If we think of God as being spirit, the Source of all life, anything that comes from God must share in the same attributes of its Creator. So therefore Christ, our true Identity, must share in all of the attributes of God. Since God is eternal, then Christ too must be eternal and can never die. If we define life as the result of the Thought of God, then anything that comes from Him must also share in those attributes. Idea and source are thus always intertwined, just as cause and effect are always intertwined, and cannot be separated. God, spirit and life are therefore one and the same.

The ego arose from the idea that it could separate from God, that it could attack God; in effect, then, the ego could choose the death of God. And when the ego chose to separate from God it also was making a choice for death, because everything in the ego's world is the exact opposite of Heaven. The ego solidified its hold on self-creation by making a phenomenal, material universe, and a body that deliberately excluded God, because the world and the body are also the exact opposite of everything that God created.

The most important characteristics of the body are that it withers, changes, decomposes and dies. So there too we see the exact same parallel that "ideas leave not their source"; the source of this world is the belief in the separation, which is the belief in the body and its death. Therefore anything that comes from that source must also share in those attributes: the idea of death has never left its source which is in the ego mind. This means that the issue or the problem is never in the idea, i.e., in the body. Rather, the problem is in the source, which is the idea of separation. Stated another way, the problem is not the body, which is but the effect of the ego thought, which is the cause. Thus, as we shall see in "The Incorruptible Body," the body does not die; the body does not do anything. It is the thought of the body that dies or that believes in death.

Q: But we still must carry that idea with us even when we leave the body, otherwise we would not come back into the body.

A: Yes, that is so. That actually is proof of the idea that the problem is not in the body, that the body may die but the thought remains with us. That is why the Course teaches later on in the text: "There is a risk in thinking death is peace." When people are fed up with this world and all the misery and suffering that is an inherent part of it, there is a very strong desire to leave this world in order to find peace. Because the problem is projected onto the body, we therefore believe if we leave the body or the world we will be free of it.

I would like to spend a little time now on workbook lesson 167, "There is one life, and that I share with God," which is almost an exact parallel to this idea that we were just talking about in the third obstacle to peace.

"There is one life, and that I share with God."

There are not different kinds of life, for life is like the truth. It does not have degrees. It is the one condition in which all that God created share. Like all His Thoughts, it has no opposite.

This is an expression of the uncompromising nature of this first level that the Course is written on. Everything that pertains to God and His extension is true; everything else is false and there is no in between, no degrees. Everything in the world of spirit is eternal; everything in the world of the body dies, and therefore is illusory. Again, there is no compromise here: You cannot have a little bit of life in this world. The entire physical world is a place of death. That is why it was made. It is a place of death where death could have a home and where God would be excluded.

There is no death because what God created shares His Life.

Again, "ideas leave not their source." What God created, namely Christ, our true Identity, must share His Life and nothing else is real.

There is no death because an opposite to God does not exist. There is no death because the Father and the Son are one.

In this world, there appears to be a state that is

life's opposite. You call it death. Yet we have learned that the idea of death takes many forms. It is the one idea which underlies all feelings that are not supremely happy.

Again, these are all very clear principles that you find throughout the three books. Another characteristic of the ego system is that it is all of one piece. You take all the ego emotions, all the negative feelings that we have in this world — anxiety, suffering, pain, depression, loss, abandonment, victimhood, mild annoyance, rage, sickness, death — all of these are but different aspects of the same idea. Once again, "Ideas leave not their source." And if we think back to the image of a funnel, the greater part of the funnel is nothing more than a projection of the neck of the funnel. And so the problem is never all the things that occur to the body; the problem is the thought of separation that gave rise to the body, and therefore gave rise to all the other seeming problems in the world.

It is the alarm to which you give response of any kind that is not perfect joy. All sorrow, loss, anxiety and suffering and pain, even a little sigh of weariness, a slight discomfort or the merest frown, acknowledge death. And thus deny you live.

This does not mean that when you find yourself wearily sighing, or having a slight feeling of dismay about something that is happening, you should feel guilty. Remember that what the Course is doing here is setting forth principles,

and helping us to understand how powerfully the
ego permeates every aspect of this world. Even if
there is the slightest twinge of annoyance or slight
displeasure about something that occurs, we are
acknowledging the body as real. We are thus believing that something, or some person outside of
ourself has affected us, has caused us pain, and
therefore we have become a victim of what other
people have done. Obviously once you begin
having thoughts like that you are right back in the
thick of the ego system. All of these ultimately
come from the one basic idea that it is possible to
kill God. It is not just that we displaced Him,
which is a mild form of the idea, it is basically that
we can destroy God.

Q: Why does this all-pervasive idea that the
world is real have such a grip on us?

A: That is a good question. I think we all have
such a strong investment in making the world
real because we share the ego's basic investment
in those three attractions of guilt, pain and death.
When we consider the fourth obstacle to peace I
will discuss this in still another way. Why is there
such resistance to the idea that God did not create
this world? Because if God did not create this
world then it means we did, which means we
could change it. But if the world is real, as the ego
maintains, then it means that ideas do leave their
source, and at that point the ego is in business.
    The principle of the Atonement rests on the as-
sumption that ideas do not leave their source. The
idea of a separated, material world of form — the

129

idea of a world in which death reigns, a world that is objective, outside and independent of the mind that conceived it — is the ego proof that ideas do leave their source. That is why we all have such a tremendous resistance to really letting that go. And yet as the Course teaches, our mind is the only place where salvation can occur, because we can change our mind about the world and its origins.

You think that death is of the body. Yet it is but an idea, irrelevant to what is seen as physical.

In other words the problem is not the body, as I have been saying, but the mind that made the body and continues to reinforce the body.

A thought is in the mind. It can be then applied as mind directs it. But its origin is where it must be changed, if change occurs.

The beginning of Chapter 21 in the text says "Seek not to change the world, but choose to change your mind about the world." True change does not come by changing behavior, or external forms. It comes from changing the underlying thinking.

 Ideas leave not their source. The emphasis this course has placed on that idea is due to its centrality in our attempts to change your mind about yourself. It is the reason you can heal. It is the cause of healing. It is why you cannot die. Its truth established you as one with God.

As I said before, the statement "ideas leave not their source" is most crucial to the Course. It is the principle of the Atonement. It explains why the separation could never have occurred. It explains why God did not create this world. It explains why everything in this world is illusory. Thus it explains why there is no order of difficulty in miracles, which we will get to a little later on, and finally it explains why we can heal. Our problems are never outside of us. Believing they are leads to hopeless depression, despair and futility, because we look out on the world in which nothing can be changed. There is no way we can change the unhappy circumstances of our own life, let alone what is going on around us in the world. And that is because we buy into the system that makes what is outside of us real, and the cause of the unhappiness that we feel.

Death is the thought that you are separate from your Creator. It is the belief conditions change, emotions alternate because of causes you cannot control, you did not make, and you can never change.

When we come to the final obstacle, The Fear of God, we will see that the same idea recurs, i.e., the belief that we are at the mercy of causes beyond our control. We will wait until then to discuss it.

It is the fixed belief ideas can leave their source, and take on qualities the source does not contain, becoming different from their own origin, apart

from it in kind as well as distance, time and form.

This is exactly what the ego wants. The ego wants our allegiance to the idea that the world is outside of our mind and does not share the attributes of the mind. Another way of stating this is that the world but mirrors exactly what is within our split ego mind.

Death cannot come from life. Ideas remain united to their source.

This is the proof that God did not create the body or this world. This is a world of death, which cannot come from life. "Ideas leave not their source." Life comes from God; death comes from the ego, and there is no compromise with that belief. Cause and effect, idea and source, are always united and cannot be separated. The ego fosters the belief that they can.

They can extend all that their source contains. In that, they can go far beyond themselves.

That is what projection does. And that is also what extension does. Extension is of God; projection is of the ego. This reflects the truth that the idea shares in all the characteristics of its source. So, for example, Christ shares in the perfection and Love of God, His Source. This is also why we can go far beyond what we believe to be ourselves in this ego state.

But they cannot give birth to what was never

given them. As they are made, so will their making be. As they were born, so will they then give birth. And where they come from, there will they return.

So the biblical statement, "For dust thou art, and unto dust shalt thou return," is true within the ego framework. Again, that is how you can see that the Old Testament creator is not God, not the true God, but the ego's god. If the idea is one of death, then everything that comes from it but must mirror death. If the thought is one of life, then everything that comes from it must mirror life.

The mind can think it sleeps, but that is all. It cannot change what is its waking state.

The Course teaches that free will does not mean we can establish what our inheritance is. It merely means we are free to choose what we believe that inheritance is. So we cannot change our inheritance as children of God, but we can change what we believe that inheritance is. We can choose to believe that we are children of the ego and not of Heaven. As the Course says, "We are at home in God dreaming of exile," meaning that we are awake in reality, but dreaming we are in exile, which obviously means that we are sleeping. Again, this is what the Atonement principle is, that the separation never really happened. We think we can change who we are, but we cannot do so in reality.

It cannot make a body nor abide within a body.

What is alien to the mind does not exist, because it has no source.

We believe we can make a body, but only in illusions; in truth we cannot. So when the Course says that "ideas leave not their source," its ultimate meaning is that there is no world because the source of that idea is the ego, which is not real. The appendix to the manual on "The Clarification of Terms" says that the ego is nothing and is nowhere.

For mind creates all things that are, and cannot give them attributes it lacks, nor change its own eternal, mindful state. It cannot make the physical. What seems to die is but the sign of mind asleep.

Just as the Bible says of Adam, this passage says that we fell asleep, and then we dreamt a bad dream, a dream of death. Once again, God, being spirit, can only create like Himself: perfect, changeless, formless and eternal. The physical world — imperfect, changeable, of form and dying — is the exact opposite, and therefore cannot have come from God.

The opposite of life can only be another form of life. As such, it can be reconciled with what created it, because it is not opposite in truth. Its form may change; it may appear to be what it is not. Yet mind is mind, awake or sleeping. It is not its opposite in anything created, nor in what it seems to make when it believes it sleeps.

God creates only mind awake. He does not

sleep, and His creations cannot share what He gives not, nor make conditions which He does not share with them.

Again, no matter what we believe we are, it ✳ does not change what we really are, because basically life does not have an opposite. This is stated at the beginning of the text: "The opposite of love is fear, but what is all-encompassing can have no opposite." Even though we seem to experience fear and death, the opposite of love and life, that experience comes from a consciousness of duality that is the framework of the world of illusion. Reality is all-encompassing and has no "other:" All is One. Life can only create life; love can only extend itself. Thus, this whole world is nothing but a dream in which there is no place for spirit which remains awake in reality.

The thought of death is not the opposite to thoughts of life. Forever unopposed by opposites of any kind, the Thoughts of God remain forever changeless, with the power to extend forever changelessly, but yet within themselves, for they are everywhere.

This is what extension is, what our creations are all about, and this process has no reference to anything in this world. God is continually extending Himself, and that extension is Christ; Christ is extending Himself, and those extensions are our creations. Yet all of them are within One Mind. There is a lovely recurring phrase near the end of the text which says of God: "He has not left His Thoughts." It is the same idea here. The

Thoughts of God (ourselves) have somehow believed, in their sleeping state, that they have left Him. And then, of course, they project that out and believe that God has left and abandoned them. In reality He has never left His Thoughts because His Thoughts have never left Him: Idea and Source remain forever united.

What seems to be the opposite of life is merely sleeping. When the mind elects to be what it is not, and to assume an alien power which it does not have, a foreign state it cannot enter, or a false condition not within its Source, it merely seems to go to sleep awhile. It dreams of time; an interval in which what seems to happen never has occurred, the changes wrought are substanceless, and all events are nowhere. When the mind awakes, it but continues as it always was.

Helen once had an image of eternity as being a solid line, and in that solid line there was a tiny, tiny, little dip, which represented the entire physical world of time. And the solid line going across — Heaven — never even knew that the dip existed, because in reality it did not. The analogue to that would be the wonderful title Joel Goldsmith gave to one of his books, *A Parenthesis in Eternity*, and that is all this world is. As real as it appears to be, it is nothing but a bad dream which was over the instant that it occurred.

The rest of this page we can omit; it is rather lovely, but it will get us away from what we are talking about here.

The Attraction of Death (concl.)

Let us go back to the bottom of page 388 and let me read those lines again.

When you accepted the Holy Spirit's purpose in place of the ego's you renounced death, exchanging it for life. We know that an idea leaves not its source. And death is the result of the thought we call the ego, as surely as life is the result of the Thought of God.

The ego's dedication is to death. And the ego's purpose is to keep us away from what the real problem is. The Course is asking us to question all the emotions, feelings and beliefs that we have, and realize that they are all coming from the same source: the decision to see ourselves as bodies, which means a decision to see ourselves as dying.

The Incorruptible Body

Let us move on now to the second section of the third obstacle, "The Incorruptible Body," on the top of page 389. Now we will get a very clear statement of what the Course is repeatedly saying about what the body is. Basically what we are seeing in all three obstacles are different forms of relating to the body: to see the body as capable of attack, the first obstacle; to see the body as valuable for what it offers, the second obstacle; to see the body as dying, the third obstacle.

From the ego came sin and guilt and death, in opposition to life and innocence, and to the Will of God Himself.

The basic thought that the ego is real produces the seeming effects of sin, guilt and death, because all of that is the opposite of the Will of God that *is* eternal life.

Where can such opposition lie but in the sick minds of the insane, dedicated to madness and set against the peace of Heaven? One thing is sure; God, Who created neither sin nor death, wills not that you be bound by them.

Nothing in this world is God's idea because He did not create it. The strange theologies that the religions of the world have fostered are all different attempts to compromise this basic principle.

There are other clever ways of trying to compromise the same principle, by saying that God does not will that we die, but He did will that the body be eternal and thus never die. It would be very possible for someone to take this phrase, "The Incorruptible Body," and misunderstand how it is used. We will get to that in a moment. The phrase "The Incorruptible Body" does not mean that the body itself is incorruptible, but that its *purpose* can be that, but not the body itself.

He knows of neither sin nor its results. The shrouded figures in the funeral procession march not in honor of their Creator, Whose Will it is they live. They are not following His Will; they are opposing it.

Nothing in this world can be seen in any way to compromise the fact that God did not create this world, despite the world's teachings. Therefore God is not present here. This world is the sole product of the imagination of the ego that thought it up, and then made up bodies which give the lying witness to the seeming fact that the ego is real.

And what is the black-draped body they would bury? A body which they dedicated to death, a symbol of corruption, a sacrifice to sin, offered to sin to feed upon and keep itself alive; a thing condemned, damned by its maker and lamented by every mourner who looks upon it as himself.

This is not a very pleasant picture of the body. Of course this does not mean that the body in and of itself is sinful, because the body in and of itself is nothing. It is the thought that gave rise to the body that is "sinful," literally meaning it is full of sin. This does not mean sinful in a sense of being evil. It is full of sin because sin is equated with separation. It is simply a mistaken thought of separation that has to be corrected.

You who believe you have condemned the Son of God to this *are* arrogant. But you who would release him are but honoring the Will of his Creator.

The ego would have us confuse humility with arrogance, and would have us believe that it is arrogant for us to assert that we are children of God and therefore are holy and can never die. Incidentally, the "him" is the Son of God, and in this case would be our brother or sister with whom we have entered into a holy relationship.

The arrogance of sin, the pride of guilt, the sepulchre of separation, all are part of your unrecognized dedication to death. The glitter of guilt you laid upon the body would kill it. For what the ego loves, it kills for its obedience. But what obeys it not, it cannot kill.

Notice the alliteration you find throughout these sections: sepulchre of separation; glitter of guilt, dedication to death. Sin is arrogant because it believes that it can attack God. And what kills the body is not the body, but what our minds have put upon the body: the decision to make the body real and to keep God out.

We can also understand our perverse fascination with the body's death as a symbolic reenactment of our insane belief that we have murdered God and Christ. And so Jesus, the perfect manifestation of the Love of God and Christ, could not be killed because he was not obeying the ego. Therefore his spiritual Self was his master, and therefore he could not be destroyed by the egos of the world around him.

You have another dedication that would keep the body incorruptible and perfect as long as it is useful for your holy purpose. The body no more dies than it can feel. It does nothing.

We can understand this to mean that the body will be incorruptible as long as the *purpose* that we give it is forgiveness, not attack. This does not mean that the physical body itself is incorruptible, as I said just before. This also means that the body does not live. To speak of the body as being eternal is a contradiction in terms. It is an attempt to compromise the metaphysical truth that is the basic premise of the Course, that God created spirit and not the body. So if the body does not live, the body does not die, because the body is literally nothing more than the projection of the thought that gave rise to it. As the text asks earlier: "Who is the you who are living in this world?"

Of itself it is neither corruptible nor incorruptible. It *is* nothing. It is the result of a tiny, mad idea of corruption that can be corrected. For God has answered this insane idea with His Own; an

Answer Which left Him not, and therefore brings the Creator to the awareness of every mind which heard His Answer and accepted it.

Recall here that the ego teaches that sin cannot be corrected; it can only be punished. The "insane idea" is the ego, and the "Answer" is the Holy Spirit, who has never left God because as an Idea in the Mind of God He has never left His Source. The Holy Spirit therefore brings the awareness and the memory of God to every mind that chooses to hear Him and follow His teaching of forgiveness.

You who are dedicated to the incorruptible have been given through your acceptance, the power to release from corruption.

The basis of this idea is found in the gospels of Matthew and John. The clearest statement is in John's gospel, the resurrection appearance in the upper room, when Jesus says to the disciples: "Those whose sins you forgive are forgiven, and those whose sins you retain are retained." The Church, as I said earlier, simply took that text as means to justify the sacrament of penance, i.e., that the priest had the power to forgive sins. This unfortunately helped contribute to the specialness attributed to the priests. I think it is quite likely, by the way, that Jesus never said those words.

However, the basic message of the statement as it is reinterpreted by the Course does makes a lot of sense. We do have the power to forgive sins, but not because of anything that is holy or special about us. We have the power to release each other — from the belief that we are sinful because it was our own mind that put the sin there in the first place. For example, if I continue to attack you, because of something you did or did not do, and you are the least bit guilty, then you will continue to feel attacked. If I forgive you, and I demonstrate your sins against me have had no effect, then I am demonstrating that they are not a cause and thus do not exist. And then they disappear. This is the gift that we give to each other, and which has the power to release from corruption. And corruption of course has nothing to do with the body; it is the corruption which is the belief in our minds that we are separate, and that this belief in separation — which is our sin — has had disastrous effects.

What better way to teach the first and fundamental principle in a course on miracles than by showing you the one that seems to be the hardest can be accomplished first?

Of course the one that would seem to be the hardest would be the overcoming of death, and here we see a reference to what Jesus himself did. That was his purpose in choosing the crucifixion as his teaching lesson, because that would seem to be the most difficult thing in all the world, since death is the most powerful witness to the ego's world.

The body can but serve your purpose. As you

look on it, so will it seem to be. Death, were it true, would be the final and complete disruption of communication, which is the ego's goal.

When we look back to the end of Chapter 15, on the bottom of page 305 which was written at Christmas, Jesus says of himself: "The Prince of Peace was born to re-establish the condition of love by teaching that communication remains unbroken even if the body is destroyed, provided that you see not the body as the necessary means of communication." That is exactly what he is talking about here. It would have seemed that the murder of Jesus would have forever stopped his communication with us. The truth, of course, was just the opposite, and just as obviously the Course would be one of the most powerful and loving witnesses to that. The fact that his body was killed had no effect on the fact that he is still with us. Therefore, he teaches in the Course that minds are joined and bodies are not, and the fact that his body was separated from us has had no effect on the fact that he is still within our minds. The responsibility then becomes ours to choose to hear his voice rather than the ego's.

Death, were it true, would be the final and complete disruption of communication, which is the ego's goal.

That is why people tried to silence Jesus two thousand years ago, and they did not succeed.

Those who fear death see not how often and

**how loudly they call to it, and bid it come to save
them from communication.**

Here is the same idea we were talking about;
we are not aware that even in the most trivial or
silly things that we feel, we are really calling to
death. We are calling to death because we believe
that it can prevent the Holy Spirit and Jesus from
communicating to us. This is another example of
the Course's understanding of the mutually exclusive relationship between God and the ego,
love and fear, life and death. Where there is the
ego, God must remain obscure; where there is
God, the ego disappears.

**For death is seen as safety, the great dark savior
from the light of truth, the answer to the Answer,
the silencer of the Voice That speaks for God.**

There is a risk in thinking death is safety. We
believe that death will free us from all the pains of
this world, and we are not aware that that one
insane thought of separation stays with us beyond the grave. As long as we believe in death in
any of its forms, major or minor, then we will
never hear the Voice of the Holy Spirit that speaks
continually to us of life.

Yet the retreat to death is not the end of conflict.

No matter how conflicted we are, dying is not
going to change the conflict that we feel. It remains with us. It is like a full suitcase that we take
along with us when the body dies, which means

we only have to come this way again, as it says in the next obstacle.

Q: The funny thing is that we do not remember this, so we come in again with a suitcase full of ignorance and forgetfulness and nothing seems to change.

A: However, on a very practical level, if you came back and had all these past memories you would be overwhelmed, and would really find it difficult to relate to the learning lessons now; whereas on another level one could understand it as the ego's attempt to keep us in darkness and ignorance, so we keep repeating the same patterns — never seeming to progress.

Only God's Answer is its end.

— None of the things in this world, up to and including death, will solve our problems or will ever really work. The only thing that will work is the Holy Spirit and His message of forgiveness.

The obstacle of your seeming love for death that peace must flow across seems to be very great. For in it lie hidden all the ego's secrets, all its strange devices for deception, all its sick ideas and weird imaginings. Here is the final end of union, the triumph of the ego's making over creation, the victory of lifelessness on Life Itself.

All of the above is what the attraction of death is. It is one of the most deeply buried and darkest of the ego's cornerstones. The belief in death contains every aspect of the ego thought system: the reality of the body, which makes the sin of separation real; and our guilt over this sin which demands our sacrifice and punishment, the ultimate of which is our death.

Under the dusty edge of its distorted world the ego would lay the Son of God, slain by its orders, proof in his decay that God Himself is powerless before the ego's might, unable to protect the life that He created against the ego's savage wish to kill.

Here is the ego's final proof that it has rendered God powerless, because He cannot save His Son. If you just think of the kind of insanity that our society upholds in terms of funerals, death and the rituals surrounding death — all of which make the body real — you can see just one of the expressions of how much we have bought the ego's lies.

Q: Many times this insanity becomes evident when whoever officiates at the funeral says that God loved this person so much that He took him back to Him.

A: Ernest Becker, a psychoanalytic sociologist, wrote an excellent book called *The Denial of Death*, which graphically describes the ego's world. The point of the book is that the major problem we all face is the need to deny our horror of death. He goes on the assumption that it is the fear of death that is the problem, not the attraction; and that we are all terribly afraid of death and seek to deny the horror of this reality. Actually, in that sense it is a very powerful treatment of how we try to deny what we have made real. We try to deny death, guilt, anger, etc. The book weakens at the end because Becker basically says that there is no way of avoiding this problem. He then states that of all the illusions the world has given us to resolve this problem, the most successful has been religion. He speaks positively about religion, not because he believes in God, but because he believes that it works the best. His treatment of the nature of the ego and guilt is, however, very powerful. It is a fine book, and won the Pulitzer Prize.

—**My brother, child of our Father, this is a *dream* of death. There is no funeral, no dark altars, no grim commandments nor twisted rituals of condemnation to which the body leads you. Ask not release of *it* (the body). But free it from the merciless and unrelenting orders you laid upon it, and forgive it what you ordered it to do.**

In other words, we made it all up, this whole dream. This is a much more sophisticated treatment of the statement Jesus makes in Chaper 2 of the text: "The correction of fear *is* your responsibility. When you ask for release from fear, you are implying that it is not. You should ask, instead, for help in the conditions that have brought the fear about. These conditions always entail a willingness to be separate. At that level you *can* help it." That is what he is saying here too: Do not ask to be released from death or all the terrible symbols of death that you made, because that is not

the problem. You ask for the release from the conditions that led to it. The conditions, as Jesus said,
are the beliefs in separation, which then translate
into our beliefs in guilt and specialness. These are
our projections onto each other. Thus what heals
us of the belief in death is our forgiveness of each
other, which we will talk about in greater depth
when we consider the final obstacle.

Q: What is meant by the grim commandments or
twisted rituals of condemnation?

A: I think you could understand this in different
ways. First of all, the language of that sentence is
the language of formal religion. It talks about altars, commandments, rituals; and certainly religions have made death real. The other level is
probably more to the point in terms of what we
are talking about here, that the "religions" of the
ego have made war real, have condoned it, and at
times have even called it holy; these "religions"
have allowed us to believe that we can condemn
other people by calling on the "justice of
Heaven," and can even devise societal rituals to
condemn people through our judicial and penal
systems, for example. All of the above attempt to
justify the belief that death is real and that murder
can be justified.

Many times the Course speaks of the ego as a
religion, an underlying thought system in which
guilt, attack and sin are sacred. But what you also
find implied in many places in the Course, and
certainly expressed here, is that the religions of
the world, especially the Western religions since

the context of the Course is Judaeo-Christian, have made the ego's basic religion into God's Word. The already cited biblical statement, "For dust thou art, and unto dust shalt thou return," is a commandment in the sense that it is God who supposedly ordains it. Thus when the ministers, priests and rabbis intone those words at a funeral, it is another way of the ego's making the body and death real.

Q: How would you view the ten commandments?

A: From a religious or societal framework, they are an attempt to list a set of prescribed behaviors, in order to control people; they are presented as coming from the mouth of God and inevitably lead to a real fear of punishment. If you break the commandments you will be punished: first castigated by the people who act as God's messengers in this world and, of course, ultimately punished by God Himself. The giveaway of what the commandments are is the emphasis on form and disregard of content. As the Course reminds us in at least two places, such disregard is one of the primary characteristics of special relationships.

In its exaltation you commanded it to die, for only death could conquer life. And what but insanity could look upon the defeat of God, and think it real?

It is referring here to the exaltation of the body by the ego. It is the insane belief that we could destroy life and God by having the body die.

Thus, the ego can proclaim that what God has created is not eternal and is destructible. The ego then places itself on the throne as God's conqueror. Therefore, the ego exalts the body, which society does by making the body something to be sought after, to be worshipped, to be venerated; the exaltation of sexuality in making the body attractive and seductive is another example of that. Such exaltation is not only with our physical body, but also with our psychological body by developing a personality which will get us what we want.

The fear of death will go as its appeal is yielded to love's real attraction.

This idea will be picked up again when we consider the fourth obstacle. When you bring the darkness to the light, the illusion to the truth, the fear to the love underneath, then the problem disappears.

The end of sin, which nestles quietly in the safety of your relationship, protected by your union with your brother, and ready to grow into a mighty force for God is very near.

Jesus is assuming that we have already advanced far, in that we have chosen forgiveness instead of guilt, holiness instead of specialness, and therefore the peace of God is right around the corner. In other passages, however, he makes it clear that the end of sin is not quite around the corner, because we still have a great deal of internal work to do.

The infancy of salvation is carefully guarded by love, preserved from every thought that would attack it, and quietly made ready to fulfill the mighty task for which it was given you.

This passage and the next paragraph have a beautiful analogue in workbook lesson 182, "I will be still an instant and go home," which talks about the Child in us, capitalized because it is referring to Christ. The text talks about the babe of Bethlehem and how Christ is reborn as a little Child anytime a wanderer chooses to leave his home. In a sense, using the metaphor of a child, Jesus is suggesting that we still have a lot of growing to do. Here too, then, he is saying that salvation is not just around the corner, at least within the illusion of time (Level Two). The text does not mean that since we have now chosen forgiveness we are finished. We still have work to do to nurture this child and let it grow. The child thus reflects our newly made decision to forgive, and it is our ongoing practice of forgiveness which will lead this child home. That is when Christ, our true Self, is restored to our awareness.

Your newborn purpose is nursed by angels, cherished by the Holy Spirit and protected by God Himself. It needs not your protection; it is *yours*. For it is deathless, and within it lies the end of death.
What danger can assail the wholly innocent? What can attack the guiltless? What fear can enter and disturb the peace of sinlessness?

The newborn purpose is the purpose of forgive-

ness, and this is going to lead us to the final obstacle. Once we choose to see our brother or sister as
ourself, and not see them as separate, that child in
us begins to grow, protected by the choice that we
made. Even if we make another choice and decide
to have a massive ego attack, there is a place
within us where that original choice is held safe
for us.

What has been given you, even in its infancy, is
in full communication with God and you. In its
tiny hands it holds, in perfect safety, every mira-
cle you will perform, held out to you. The mira-
cle of life is ageless, born in time but nourished
in eternity. Behold this infant, to whom you gave
a resting place by your forgiveness of your
brother, and see in it the Will of God. Here is the
babe of Bethlehem reborn. And everyone who
gives him shelter will follow him, not to the
cross, but to the resurrection and the life.

Here, obviously, Jesus is making reference to
the imagery of Christmas. However, he is not
talking about himself but the Christ in us, of
whom he is the greatest symbol. It is the Holy
Spirit who is the communication link between
Christ and ourselves — the link between our Self
in Heaven and the ego self that we believe is here.
The "resurrection and the life" is taken from
John's gospel. The author of the gospel has
shifted the meaning of the resurrection from the
physical resurrection of Jesus on Easter, as it was
given in the other three gospels, to a more spiritual experience. This gospel speaks of our being

153

reborn by accepting Jesus and the meaning of his life into our minds and hearts. This is closer to the Course's view, which sees the resurrection as the reawakening from the dream of death, a total change of mind that comes through forgiveness.

Q: Would this be similar to the Second Coming?

A: If you spell it in lower case. When the Course talks about the Second Coming in capital letters it is really talking about the reawakening of the whole Sonship; but here we can think of it as the second coming in each of us as we begin to choose to awaken. But by using the image of a child, Jesus certainly does express, once again, that this is a process; we have to nurture and nourish this child. And even though the outcome is as certain as God, which means that the decision is protected by the angels — obviously a symbol here — it still necessitates a tremendous amount of work on our part. It is a decision to forgive that has to be chosen over and over again, and there will certainly be many, many times when we will make the other choice. So we are still really talking about the beginnings of salvation, the beginnings of a process.

When anything seems to you to be a source of fear, when any situation strikes you with terror and makes your body tremble and the cold sweat of fear comes over it, remember it is always for *one* reason; the ego has perceived it as a symbol of fear, a sign of sin and death.

Whenever anything really upsets us in the

world we should realize that what is upsetting us is that we have made the upsetting thing into a symbol. It is not the thing itself which is upsetting us, not what we are seeing in our or another person's body; what is upsetting us is an interpretation that we have made on these bodies. Looking at Chart A it becomes apparent that what is upsetting us is not what we see here on the right-hand side, in the world, but a decision we have chosen in our mind to perceive through the eyes of the ego and the eyes of fear.

Remember, then, that neither sign nor symbol should be confused with source, for they must stand for something other than themselves.

Again, it is the same idea in that what we are seeing out here in the world, on the right-hand side of Chart A, is not the problem. The problem is the source of what we have seen, and that source always rises within our mind in a decision here on the left-hand side of the chart to see ourselves as egos rather than as Christ.

Their meaning cannot lie in them, but must be sought in what they represent.

And they, sign or symbol, can only represent one of two things. Either they represent the fear of the ego, the symbol of death that is the ego's thought system, or they represent and symbolize the forgiveness that the Holy Spirit holds in our minds. Again, it is never the signs or symbols in and of themselves. The workbook says at the beginning, "I am never upset for the reason I think," because it is always the meaning we have given to the sign or symbol that is upsetting us, and not the sign or symbol itself.

And they may thus mean everything or nothing, according to the truth or falsity of the idea which they reflect.

If we choose to see through the eyes of Christ, the perception of the Holy Spirit, then we see everything through the mind's eye, and that is truth; if we see through the eyes of the ego then we see nothing, and that is the illusion or the falsity.

Confronted with such seeming uncertainty of meaning, judge it not.

This is what the Course means by not judging. We simply cannot comprehend or pretend that we know the meaning of what we behold; we really do not understand what is going on in our lives, the lives of those we live with, or the lives of the people in the world. Therefore we should not judge what we are perceiving, but should recognize that we do not understand what it means.

Remember the holy presence of the One given to you to be the Source of judgment. Give it to Him to judge for you, and say:
"Take this from me and look upon it, judging it for me.
Let me not see it as a sign of sin and death, nor use it for destruction.

> *Teach me how **not** to make of it an obstacle to peace.*
> *But let You use it for me, to facilitate its coming."*

Again, I think this is a very clear statement of a basic principle of the Course process. There is no question that on our own all of this would be totally inconceivable and impossible to accomplish, since there is no way that we could change our thinking or even change the world we behold. All that the Course is saying to us is that when we are tempted to be upset by anything, when anything seems to be a source of fear, what we do is recognize that we have judged it wrongly and have made it into a symbol of attack, sin and fear. At that instant of recognition we call upon the Holy Spirit and ask Him to judge it for us. He would see it as a mistake in our perception that has to be corrected. If we perceive people doing something that is hateful and of the ego, then He would teach us that they are also calling out for help just as we are, and we are joined with them in that call. He would remind us not to use it as an obstacle to peace by making guilt, pain or death real. Furthermore, if we turn the problem over to the Holy Spirit the upset becomes not an obstacle to peace but a facilitator of peace. The problem becomes the opportunity He uses to correct our misperceptions of what we have seen outside of us and how we have seen ourselves. That is how the world will be healed.

Q: I am wondering — is it implied in these obstacles that we confront them chronologically in our path like the layers of an onion?

A: In one sense I think it is. We will go through a chart in a minute which will suggest this. The process obviously is not in strict chronological sequence any more than the six stages of trust in the manual are a strict sequence, but it does suggest a layered effect, which can occur simultaneously on different levels. For example, it is easy for us to get angry, and the first obstacle describes our desire to get rid of peace. The second obstacle is the attraction of pain and the whole worshipping of the body, the third obstacle is the attraction of death. So in some sense it is almost like getting deeper and deeper into the system until the final obstacle is reached, which we are now about to do, and that is the fear of God. Again, you have to be careful not to make it into a strict pattern, and realize in the final analysis that they are simultaneously different ways of making the body real. As I mentioned earlier, this is really what this whole series of obstacles is about: the different ways of manifesting the seeming reality of the body, through attack, pain, and utimately through death.

Chart B

Before we move ahead to the fourth and final obstacle, "The Fear of God," let us look at Chart B, which will encapsulate all four obstacles to peace. Briefly reviewing the basic schematic here, we begin on the left-hand side with God and Christ, who are joined in spirit and, of course, are joined in love. Then the separation seems to occur, which is that solid line at the top going across the page. This is the origin of the ego, the idea that we have separated from God, destroyed Him, and set ourselves up on the throne of creation. This is the content of the dream.

At the moment that the separation seemed to occur, God extended Himself into the dream, and that is indicated by the solid line going downwards to the bottom of the page. That extension is called the Holy Spirit, who was then placed in our mind. He becomes the place deep within us where He is always speaking to us of the Love of God. It is this place that the ego is most afraid of, because the ego now realizes that if we ever hear the Voice of the Holy Spirit, He would tell us that the whole thing is a dream. As is described earlier in the text, "He is the Call to awaken and be glad," because He is the Call of joy that informs us that this world is nothing but a bad dream. Since we cannot change what God has established as reality, the Holy Spirit urges us to return to the home that we have never truly left. That is the ego's real fear. There is a very powerful section in Chapter 13 called "The Fear of Redemption," which makes this point very clearly. It states that we believe we are afraid of crucifixion, punishment and pain, but what we are really afraid of is redemption. We are afraid of getting back to this place here at the bottom right-hand side of Chart B, where love and the memory of God are held for us by the Holy Spirit.

This love, then, is the ego's real fear, and it is the ego's main goal to blot the Holy Spirit out of our awareness, for if we hear His Voice the ego will disappear. Through subterfuge the ego tells us that we should be afraid to ever get too close to God (the Holy Spirit) for He would destroy us. So looking at Chart B, the second layer above the Presence of Love and memory of God is the fear of God and Love. This becomes the ego's first line of defense which teaches us not to get too close to love, because it will crucify and destroy us. Christianity, based on the Bible, incorporated this insane ego thought system into a theology of God demanding the crucifixion of His only Son, whom He loved, because we were sinful. So, the ego reasons for us, if God crucified Jesus whom He loved, what will He do to the rest of us, whom He could not possibly love as much because of our sins against Him? You can see here how Christian theology became a perfect mirror of the ego system. Two lovely lines in one of Helen's poems, "Amen," refute this insanity: "Love does not crucify. It only saves. . . . . God does not crucify. He merely is."

What is important to remember here is that because the ego teaches us that God's Love *does* crucify, we should therefore be afraid of this Love. The ego now sets up a barricade through which we will never pass, so it hopes, because if we pass through that barricade we will realize that God is not fear but Love. The real fear of God in the ego system, then, is the recognition that if we let God into our mind the ego is finished. For example, if we sit in a dark room and switch on a light, the darkness disappears. When the first letter of John says "Perfect love casts out fear," it is the same idea. The ego knows if we allow ourselves to be in the presence of perfect Love through the Holy Spirit, the ego is finished. That is the ego's fear of God.

However, the ego camouflages its real fear by telling us that God is not love but fear, because He will destroy us. There are many passages in the text and workbook which describe how the ego projects itself onto God, getting everything upside down. Thus the attributes of the ego — fear, guilt, punishment and death — are projected onto God, and it is seen as His Will that we suffer, sacrifice and die.

Now that the ego has built its first line of defense, teaching us that **we** should be afraid of God, it superimposes further defenses. It tells us that we cannot get too close to God because we would be destroyed. Therefore we have to keep protecting ourselves against our Creator by erecting more and more citadels against Him. These citadels are what the Course refers to as special relationships, which are all different aspects of the dream.

In the section called "The 'Hero' of the Dream" in Chapter 27, the same basic material is talked about. The body is the hero of the dream and, referring to Chart B, the body is the entire box on the lower right-hand side of the page: a dream of the reality of this world. The world then becomes the screen onto which the ego projects itself and a place where the ego hides. And the more we feel that our problems are in this box, whether they are problems of attack, pain or death in any form, the further we are getting from what the ego tells us is the real fear, the fear of God; and if we are not able to approach that fear then we cannot penetrate it to what is the ego's *real* fear: the fact that God does not destroy; He simply loves us.

We are thus talking about one distraction after another, one camouflage after another, one line of defense superimposed upon another line of defense, so that we get further and further away from the real problem. And that is another reason why we all have such a tremendous attraction to this world. It is an attraction to the "reality" of the dream, because we identify with the ego's need to keep us from the reality of what we are most afraid of: remembering that we are all one with God and have never left Him. So what we do is construct layers upon layers of defenses. We have more and more dreams of being a victim, which we saw in the first three obstacles to peace, i.e., different ways to experience ourselves as victims, all of which justify our belief in attack and making others victims in return.

PART IV:
THE FOURTH OBSTACLE

The Fourth Obstacle:
The Fear of God

Here in the fourth and final obstacle the Course is assuming that we have worked our way through the other three. We stand before the final obstacle, the fear of God, and that is the most terrifying one of all because the ego has convinced us that God wants to destroy us. On the one hand the ego tells us that we have destroyed God, but on the other hand it knows that God cannot be destroyed. Therefore the ego changes Him from a God of Love to a god of vengeance who is out for our blood. First this wrathful Father demanded Jesus' blood, and now He demands everyone else's. Sometimes, too, Jesus is seen in the same light, when he becomes the harsh judge who will punish us for our sins. This then is the basic paradigm we find in these obstacles. What makes them so powerful as defenses is that the ego tells us that they will protect us from God's destruction of us, which is what we as egos are really most afraid of.

What would you see without the fear of death? What would you feel and think if death held no attraction for you? Very simply, you would remember your Father. The Creator of life, the Source of everything that lives, the Father of the universe and of the universe of universes, and of everything that lies even beyond them would you remember.

165

A basic formula that appears in many different places in the Course is that our task is to see the face of Christ in our brother, and then remember God. To see the face of Christ in someone else is certainly not to see the face of Jesus; it is not talking about a physical face at all. The face of Christ is the Course's symbol of innocence and forgiveness. I see the face of Christ in you because I look beyond the darkness of your ego. At that point the ego system is undone, through forgiveness, and what is left is the memory of God. That succinct formula encapsulates the entire process: We see the face of Christ in each other and then we remember God. Incidentally, the Course uses the word "universe" in different ways. In the above passage it is referring to the infinite universe of spirit.

And as this memory rises in your mind, peace must still surmount a final obstacle, after which is salvation completed, and the Son of God entirely restored to sanity. For here your world *does* end.

As we work through the fear and attraction of death, the memory of God will start to glimmer in our consciousness. That is when the final obstacle rears its ugly head. Suddenly this loving God begins to rise in our mind, and the ego turns full force on us and says, "You had better watch it, God will destroy you." Here is another example of the ego's viciousness talked about elsewhere by the Course. Very often when we are on the brink of really remembering who we are, remembering our spiritual Self and true function in this world, the ego really tries to do us in. At that point it gets vicious, not only toward ourselves but toward other people. One of the ways you can sometimes tell if you are getting close to God is when you begin to feel desperate, and you feel tremendous surges of hatred and grievances rising up within you.

In mystical literature you can find many examples of this paradox, such as St. John of the Cross' references to "The Dark Night of the Soul," which was for him the penultimate step along the spiritual path. It is after the Dark Night that one reaches the experience of union with God. It comes when we have worked through these other layers of defenses and nothing remains except ourselves and God. That is when the ego teaches that we are finished because, in fact, *it* is finished. That is when the viciousness comes.

The fourth obstacle to be surmounted hangs like a heavy veil before the face of Christ. Yet as His face rises beyond it, shining with joy because He is in His Father's Love, peace will lightly brush the veil aside and run to meet Him, and to join with Him at last.

Jesus here says, "peace will lightly brush the veil aside," but remember that he is looking at this from the other side of the veil, where the veil is seen as nothing. On the side that we are on, however, as the Course says later, the veil seems to be quite heavy and painful to confront.

For this dark veil, which seems to make the face of Christ Himself like to a leper's, and the bright rays of His Father's Love that light His face with glory appear as streams of blood, fades in the blazing light beyond it when the fear of death is gone.

These are wonderful lines, filled with poetic imagery. The first part, "this dark veil which seems to make the face of Christ Himself like to a leper's," is one of the places in the Course which refers to the scene in "Hamlet" when the Prince holds up the picture of his dead father, Claudius, comparing it with the picture of his uncle who is his father's murderer. Earlier in the play Hamlet compares the two men to Hyperion and a satyr, Hamlet identifying his father to the god Jupiter, and his uncle to a satyr or devil. The reference here is also to the section "The Two Pictures" in Chapter 17.

This is the darkest veil, upheld by the belief in death and protected by its attraction.

What keeps us from ever having to deal with this "darkest veil" is the third obstacle. If you recall the right-hand side of Chart B, each of the defensive layers has as its purpose to "protect" us from what is immediately beneath it. The deeper we go, the more powerful and vicious the defense. Thus, the purpose of the attraction of death is to keep us from penetrating still further to the final defense — the fear of God.

The dedication to death and to its sovereignty is

but the solemn vow, the promise made in secret to the ego never to lift this veil, not to approach it, nor even to suspect that it is there.

This idea, discussed in the next page as well, is that we have made a vow to the ego, which now feels betrayed and justified in its viciousness. We made a vow to the ego never to look beyond this veil and realize that God is simply Love. We made a vow never to penetrate this final obstacle.

This is the secret bargain made with the ego to keep what lies beyond the veil forever blotted out and unremembered.

We have all made this secret vow or bargain with the ego, which is upheld over and over again in our special relationships. Our decisions to see ourselves as victims and unfairly treated, our decisions to attack and hate, to feel rejected, abandoned, let down and betrayed, are all but different expressions of a bargain we made with the ego. In summary, we promised the ego that we would never move beyond the defenses of the dream — all the special relationships in which we perceived ourselves as victims — and ultimately never get beyond the final veil, the fear of God.

Here is your promise never to allow union to call you out of separation (which is never to allow forgiveness to undo specialness); the great amnesia in which the memory of God seems quite forgotten; the cleavage of your Self from you; — *the fear of God*, the final step in your dissociation.

Dissociation is a process of splitting off within ourselves. What we have ultimately split off is our true Self, the extension of God's Love. We have split that Self off from everything else, and then have forgotten we have done so.

See how the belief in death would seem to "save" you.

If we believe in death in any form we never have to get beneath it to the fear of God. That is an even more powerful reason why we are so attracted to death and to the body: that is what the ego tells us will protect us from the horrifying fear that God would destroy us.

For if this were gone, what could you fear but life? It is the attraction of death that makes life seem to be ugly, cruel and tyrannical. You are no more afraid of death than of the ego.

The word "life" here would be a synonym for God. Again, it is not the fear of death that is the defense, but rather the attraction to it.

These are your chosen friends. For in your secret alliance with them you have agreed never to let the fear of God be lifted, so you could look upon the face of Christ and join Him in His Father.

All of the above is what we have actively chosen. This is what the Course is saying over and over again. This is such a key concept in terms of understanding its whole thought system. Since we actively choose to remain in this dream, a

dream of attack, separation and death, we are terrified of this fear of God, that God will punish us.
But at the same time we are attracted even to that,
because it is the ego's attraction to keep God, the
real God, away from us.

Q: Are you implying that this secret alliance with
the ego, once chosen, is quickly repressed into the
unconscious, and then we make believe we have
no alternative choice?

A: Yes, that is exactly what we have done, and
then believe it is done to us. We are still allying
ourselves with sin, guilt, attack, fear and ultimately death. But the whole idea is that we have
chosen this and are still choosing this. The purpose of the ego system is to teach us that we are
the victims of the world. Yet these are *dreams* of
victimhood; in truth we are not victims of the
world but "victims" of our own thinking: the decision to continually prove to ourselves that God
is cruel. And that is the alliance. Each of us who
walks this earth makes that pact with each other.
There are sections later on in the text that specifically treat these secret vows we have made.

**Every obstacle that peace must flow across is
surmounted in just the same way; the fear that
raised it yields to the love beyond, and so the
fear is gone.**

That is what we talked about before, bringing
the darkness to the light.

Forgive me an analogy to Beethoven: His greatest symphony is his ninth, in four movements. In

the beginning of the final movement Beethoven quotes briefly from each of the preceding three movements, as a way of bringing back to us the experience of those movements; and then he summarily rejects them in a powerful musical phrase. Beethoven is saying to us that it is not these earlier sounds; listen now to this last movement. Then you hear the lovely melodic theme of "The Ode to Joy," which becomes the seed for the final movement. I think that is exactly what Jesus is doing here. He brings back now in specific brief statements the preceding three obstacles, and that is what gives rise to the fourth:

And so it is with this. (Now you see the three preceding obstacles. The first obstacle:) **The desire to get rid of peace and drive the Holy Spirit from you fades in the presence of the quiet recognition that you love Him.**

The desire to get rid of peace is to hold a speck of grievances or hatred against someone else, but we realize that we do not really want to drive the Holy Spirit away: We love Him. Now the second obstacle:

The exaltation of the body is given up in favor of the spirit, which you love as you could never love the body.

In all of these now we bring the fear and the hatred to the love and the love dissipates the fear. And the third obstacle:

And the appeal of death is lost forever as love's attraction stirs and calls to you. From beyond

each of the obstacles to love, Love Itself has
called. And each has been surmounted by the
power of the attraction of what lies beyond. Your
wanting fear seemed to be holding them in
place.

We are continually choosing fear, the final obstacle, and that is what held in place our beliefs in
the preceding three obstacles.

Yet when you heard the Voice of Love beyond
them, you answered and they disappeared.

Specifically Jesus is saying here that whenever
we feel tempted to attack somebody, to worship
pleasure and/or pain, and to worship death, we
should realize that these are all choices to put obstacles and barriers between ourselves and God.
If we just remind ourselves of His Love and His
Presence in our lives, and not only His Love for
us but ours for Him, then all of these seeming
obstacles will just disappear. That is the ego's
fear. Because deep within us the ego must know
that if we really turn to Jesus and accept his love,
all of this will go; even and including the final obstacle which is the fear that this loving, gentle,
and peaceful Voice will destroy us.

Q: Since most of the guilt and fear are unconscious, how many of the almost five billion people
on this planet know this?

A: Not very many. That is why there is a plan of
teachers, as he says in the manual. The purpose
of the Course is to help more and more people

change their minds, and then begin to become instruments of peace and love in the world. I do not think this is going to happen in our lifetime, but the foundation of the plan will begin now. The aim of the Course is to train people to do what it is saying, not just superficially, not just behaviorally, but through a profound mind change that sees no attack in anyone, no justification for separation anywhere, and sees only that all people are joined in calling for the Love of God. That is the only way that peace will come into the world. It cannot come from without; it can only come from within.

Our position now is that we have gone through the other three obstacles: the belief in anger, pain and death. All were just defenses that we chose because we were even more afraid of this last one. As we have seen, we *believe* we are afraid of hatred, pain and death; but we are really attracted to them because we are even more afraid of the last obstacle, the fear of God. The following are two very powerful paragraphs.

And now you stand in terror before what you swore never to look upon.

If anyone ever tells you that this is a nice and easy path, and why do you exaggerate the negatives, you just have to read passages like this, "And now you stand in terror. . . ." There is no one on this earth who is not terrified of the punishment that will come because we are here, in the body and the world.

Your eyes look down, remembering your promise to your "friends." (It is going to repeat again the idea of the first three obstacles. These are our friends, the allies we chose to shield and protect us from the destruction by God.) **The "loveliness" of sin, the delicate appeal of guilt, the "holy" waxen image of death, and the fear of vengeance of the ego you swore in blood not to desert, all rise and bid you not to raise your eyes. For you realize that if you look on this and let the veil be lifted, *they* will be gone forever. All of your "friends," your "protectors" and your "home" will vanish. Nothing that you remember now will you remember.**

The Course says that when we all heal our minds and leave this world, we will not remember anything because the whole thing will disappear. That eye blink or parenthesis in eternity I mentioned earlier will simply disappear. It is not that we would think back on what things were like, since everything would be gone completely. It would be the same as when you awaken from a dream and within a few seconds the dream leaves you. Recall that this is the same idea, not expressed as poetically as it is here, that we find in the section on the "Fear of Redemption," which says that we are really afraid that if we leave all this behind we shall leap into our Father's arms. We shall discuss that section a little later.

Q: Could you explain the line, "the fear of vengeance of the ego"?

A: In the ego system the vengeance of the ego is

projected onto God, and thus becomes the vengeance of God. All those terrible, vengeful passages in the Bible are an example of that. It has nothing to do with the living God, but is the vengeance of the ego projected onto God. And yet that is the same ego — that we have sworn never to desert — that will heap vengeance on us. That is what makes this whole system so unbelievably insane.

Let me recapitulate the ideas in systematic order. We pledge our fidelity to this ego — a thought of vengeance — because somehow in the insanity of it all we believe that the ego will protect us from the vengeance of God, which is really the disguised vengeance of the ego. We can understand why the world is such a hopelessly depressing and despairing place. In the ego system there is no way out; the world is just a place of continuing vengeance.

It seems to you the world will utterly abandon you if you but raise your eyes.

That is the ego in us that would believe this. People have said if they really practice this Course their life will be dull and boring, and there will be no excitement. Yet all that will happen is that the ego's allies — guilt, attack, suffering, sickness, despair, depression and death — will no longer be here.

Yet all that will occur is you will leave the world forever. This is the re-establishment of *your* will.

Many times the Course talks about how our will

is one with God's. The ego believes that the wills are opposite, because the ego is opposite to God. Therefore since the ego is the belief that the ego is the opposite of God's Will, if we identify as an ego, then we must also be in opposition to God's Will. So the Course is continually saying to us that God's Will and our will are one and the same.

Look upon it, open-eyed, and you will nevermore believe that you are at the mercy of things beyond you, forces you cannot control, and thoughts that come to you against your will.

This is what we talked about in our discussion of workbook lesson 167. One of the key ideas in this dream is that we are at the mercy of things beyond us; i.e., we are the victims of the world. For example, we believe we are the victims of our parents at birth and how they have mistreated us; how the world mistreats us: the churches and synogogues, the government, our spouses, children, friends, teachers — everyone has mistreated us, including Jesus and God, and there is nothing we can do about it. Once we can get beyond these grievances, we are also getting beyond the fear that God will victimize us. The key to understanding what made the entire separation so real to us is our belief that we have attacked and victimized God, and since we project that attack out, it now appears as if God victimizes us. This is the dynamic that teaches us that God is to be feared. Then we take this dynamic and project it over and over again to all of our relationships, believing that the world victimizes us. Once we truly let all of this go, we see that God is not victimizing us at all. The belief in that dynamic disappears as we realize finally that we had only been at the mercy of our own thoughts, and now those thoughts are gone.

It *is* your will to look on this. No mad desire, no trivial impulse to forget again, no stab of fear nor the cold sweat of seeming death can stand against your will. For what attracts you from beyond the veil is also deep within you, unseparated from it and completely one.

At some point we will know with certainty that the Love of God that calls us is not something that is alien to us. It is who we really are. The Holy Spirit speaks in that part of our mind, the right mind, that we have forgotten and have dissociated from. Once again, our will and God's are one and the same.

One final point before we go on to "The Lifting of the Veil": It would be the experience of all people here that they are at the mercy of forces beyond their control. The reason this is such a compelling witness to us, and seems so real, is that we identify with the body. For example, if we only identify as a body, and the weather suddenly shifts and becomes frigid, we will experience ourself as a victim of the cold; or if we are driving a car on the highway and all at once there is an accident in which we plow into the car in front of us, and the car in back plows into us, it would seem again as if we are at the mercy of forces beyond our control. That is how it appears within the world of the dream and the body.

Remember that these obstacles to peace are talking about different ways that we identify with the body as an instrument of attack, as a source of pleasure and, therefore, as a source of pain, and finally as the victim of death. The ego tells us that the body will be destroyed by this vengeful God, whom we should fear. Once we can remember clearly that we are not bodies, then we can also remember that it is not our true Selves that are being attacked. That was Jesus' message on the cross. His body appeared to be murdered, and it certainly seemed to be at the mercy of forces beyond his control, yet what he taught was that he was not his body. So while his body seemed to be attacked, Jesus did not experience it that way because he did not identify himself with the body. Furthermore, because he chose through the crucifixion to teach his lesson of love, Jesus was not at the mercy of forces beyond his control.

If something happens to your body, or to the bodies of those whom you love or those with whom you identify, the lesson is first, not to deny that the event occurred. What you deny is the interpretation that you have placed on the event, namely that you have been victimized. The rallying cry of the ego is: "Why is this always happening to me?" And within the world of the body that is how it appears. The trick is not to deny what seems to happen, but to deny the ego's interpretation that it is victimizing you. You can only be a victim if you see yourself as a body and someone else as a body.

The same idea is expressed in "The Responsibility for Sight" in Chapter 21:

This is the only thing that you need do for vision, happiness, release from pain and the complete escape from sin, all to be given you. Say only this, but mean it with no reservations, for here the power of salvation lies:

I am responsible for what I see.
I choose the feelings I experience, and I decide
upon the goal I would achieve.
And everything that seems to happen to me
I ask for, and receive as I have asked.

Deceive yourself no longer that you are helpless in the face of what is done to you. Acknowledge but that you have been mistaken, and all effects of your mistakes will disappear.

It is impossible the Son of God be merely driven by events outside of him. It is impossible that happenings that come to him were not his choice. His power of decision is the determiner of every situation in which he seems to find himself by chance or accident.

This important passage can be understood on two levels. The first is to shift our interpretation of the situation from one in which we are the victim, to one which is a classroom in which we learn the lesson of forgiveness that we are not a victim of the world we see, as the workbook teaches. The second level, the metaphysical, is where we recognize that there are no accidents, and that this is a situation we have chosen from another dimension of our mind.

When we realize that our body is merely a learning device to teach us that the dream of victimhood, the dream of the separation, is an illusion and nothing more than a dream, then the body will appear totally different. And then we will not see it as having victimized us; or other bodies as victimizing us; we will see the body as providing an opportunity whereby we could learn that our separation from God has had no effects. Therefore our separation from the world and the people in our world has also had no effects. That is what the message of Jesus was.

These sections, incidentally, are leading up to Easter. There are references to Easter in "The Lifting of the Veil," and the first section of Chapter 20 was written on Palm Sunday. You can see very clearly how the message of Easter and the resurrection becomes interwoven here. It is a message that teaches us that we are not the body, which means we are not victims of the world but only, as we have seen, victims of our own thoughts.

The Lifting of the Veil (beg.)

Now we come to "The Lifting of the Veil"
which is the final section in "The Obstacles to
Peace." This is a particularly interesting section as
well as being one of the most beautiful in the
book. It is another indication of how the Course
blends its metaphysical teaching with a profound
practicality. We ended up in the fourth obstacle,
"The Fear of God," talking about the fact that we
are all terrified of the God who would destroy us,
and how the different aspects of the ego's
thought system have become our allies in our war
against God. In this final section Jesus shifts to
the perfect solution to this problem: forgiveness.
We find here a beautiful description of what it
means to choose and have a holy relationship.

The preceding section ended with this sentence: "For what attracts you from beyond the
veil is also deep within you, unseparated from it
and completely one." What is deepest within us
is the Love of God, and it is this Love that is the
most frightening to the ego. Before we begin with
"The Lifting of the Veil," however, I thought we
would do a particularly important section in
Chapter 13, "The Fear of Redemption," which in
many ways parallels this final obstacle, even
though it comes six chapters earlier. It very powerfully explains why we are so afraid of God. Re-
freshing our memory with Chart B, which I will
refer to frequently in this section, the bottom part

of the right-hand box represents the aspect of our mind where God's Love is present through the Holy Spirit. The ego's fear of this Love is the main theme of this section.

The Fear of Redemption

You may wonder why it is so crucial that you look upon your hatred and realize its full extent. You may also think that it would be easy enough for the Holy Spirit to show it to you, and to dispel it without the need for you to raise it to awareness yourself.

One of the things that the Course strongly emphasizes is that we really have to look on this ego system that we have made. Chapter 13, the longest one in the book, is where the greatest discussion of guilt occurs. It is also a very powerful precursor to the sections in Chapter 15 on special relationships. Those and subsequent sections on special relationships, being the most difficult in the book to get through because of what they tell us about ourselves, also become a very important witness to this first statement. How essential it is that we realize just how filled with hatred our ego selves are! Until we do so we cannot change our mind. We all have this magical belief that somehow the Holy Spirit can heal this hatred, these deeper layers of our ego system, without doing our homework. We want Him to do the work so we do not have to confront what we are so terrified of. Obviously, this is not the way salvation works. The text now explains to us exactly why it does not work.

Yet there is one more obstacle you have interposed between yourself and the Atonement. (This obstacle really is the final obstacle we have been considering, The Fear of God.) **We have said that no one will countenance fear if he recognizes it. Yet in your disordered state of mind you are not afraid of fear. You do not like it, but it is not your desire to attack that really frightens you.**

The ego teaches us that we should be afraid of everything in the world, because we deserve to be attacked because of what we have done. So from our fear of being attacked by others we move one step lower, which is the fear of this attack because of what we believe we have done. This is what lies in the individual consciousness of all of us. Beneath this, however, is the fear that God Himself will attack us because we believe we have attacked Him. This is the original meaning of sin and fear: We believe we have sinned against God by attacking Him, attested to by our guilt, which then tells us that we deserve to be punished; and thus we stand in terror of this inevitable punishment. But the Course is explaining to us that this punishment is not what we are really afraid of, for it is only a smoke screen.

You are not seriously disturbed by your hostility. You keep it hidden because you are more afraid of what it covers.

The ego has very cleverly built up a massive smoke screen to distract us from what the problem really is. Almost everybody in our world has some problem or another with anger. Either we fear destroying other people because of the force of it or, more to the point, we believe that becoming angry is a bad thing. Somehow we think nice, holy people do not get angry. Thus we invest a tremendous amount of time and energy in dealing with this problem. Unfortunately, psychology has not been very helpful because it has fallen into the ego's trap of teaching us that anger is something that is natural and even desired. The ego has thus confused us about where the problem really is. It tells us that the problem is not that God will destroy us. We keep that fear hidden because it hides something that we are even more afraid of.

You could look even upon the ego's darkest cornerstone without fear if you did not believe that, without the ego, you would find within yourself something you fear even more.

This is an aspect of the Course's thought system which I think is unique in spiritual literature. The idea is that it is not anything on the right-hand side of Chart B that we are afraid of at all, except the very bottom which is love and the memory of God. Everything else is merely a smoke screen that we feel called upon to use as defenses, but they are not the problem. We even can "look upon the ego's darkest cornerstone," which is that we have separated from God. However the real reason we do not look is that we are even more afraid of what lies underneath. Here comes the clinching line:

You are not really afraid of crucifixion (which is the Course's symbol of the ego's punishment for our sinfulness). **Your real terror is of redemption.**

Here is the real fear of God, and this is the final obstacle to peace: We really do not fear that God will attack us; we fear that He will not! The ego's fear is that we love God and that He loves us eternally.

Under the ego's dark foundation is the memory of God, and it is of this that you are really afraid. For this memory would instantly restore you to your proper place, and it is this place that you have sought to leave.

This all makes very good sense when you keep in mind that the entire thought system of the ego is predicated on the belief that God is absent — or if God is present, that He is a cruel and punishing God. If it can be revealed to us that God is Love, then the ego is out of business. And *that* is the ego's fear. To the extent that we identify with the ego's thought system we also identify with that fear, which then needs to be defended against, represented by the various defenses on the right-hand side of Chart B. All the different dreams of victimhood are what we believe will defend us against the ego's insane idea that God would hurt us. Sanity, however, is not that God would hurt us, but that He loves us.

Your fear of attack is nothing compared to your fear of love. You would be willing to look even

upon your savage wish to kill God's Son, if you did not believe that it saves you from love.

Even though our ego consciousness would try to convince us that more than anything else we want someone to love us, most of us can identify with the idea that sometimes what we are most afraid of is that certain people would get too close to us. For when someone does get really close, or we allow ourselves to get close to someone else, or even when things begin working out in our lives, there is a part of us which, unconsciously and sometimes even consciously, tries to sabotage it. That is our ego, afraid of love and afraid of our remembering who we really are.

For this wish (this is the savage wish to kill God's Son which is what the separation was) **caused the separation, and you have protected it because you do not want the separation healed. You realize that, by removing the dark cloud that obscures it, your love for your Father would impel you to answer His call and leap into Heaven. You believe that attack is salvation because it would prevent you from this.**

Therefore it is the ego in us that does not want the separation healed. In essence the Course is teaching us that every single concern in this world is an illusion. That is what the workbook means when it says that we are never upset for the reason we think. We are only upset because we believe we have separated from God. Moreover, underneath that belief is the ego's awareness that the separation is all made-up and hence a lie. So that all of our seeming problems in the world can be traced back to the original belief in sin and separation, which is also an ego smoke screen, obscuring the fact that it never happened in reality.

The presence of the Holy Spirit in our mind is a continual reminder that we can never truly separate ourselves from God, our Source. That is what the Course means elsewhere when it says that no one could ever be totally insane, because there is always a part of our mind that contains the Holy Spirit. Obviously we often feel as if we are insane, with the Holy Spirit seeming to be inaccessible to us. But somewhere deep within us He is present, which means that somewhere deep within us is God's Love. And that is what we as egos are afraid of, making everything else in the world — without exception — a defense against that.

When we discuss "The Lifting of the Veil" this will become even clearer. Practically no one in this world is in touch with the fear of God's Love. Nevertheless, we are in touch with our fear of each other: all our special relationships — the hurts and angers, the petty hates and bitternesses, and the dreams of deprivation and victimhood. If we look at each and every one of these and realize it is made up, then we would be able to be led through that final veil.

For still deeper than the ego's foundation, and much stronger than it will ever be, is your intense and burning love of God, and His for you. This is what you really want to hide.

In honesty, is it not harder for you to say "I love" than "I hate?"

In our world, certainly, it is much easier to hate people and feel justified in this hatred, than it is to truly love someone. This is not the love that specialness holds dear, but the love that does not see another as separate from ourselves; not seeing a person's interests as separate, or more or less important than our own, and having no expectations of anyone.

You associate love with weakness and hatred with strength, and your own real power seems to you as your real weakness.

This is another example of the dichotomy that the Course makes which ultimately is based on a line from St. Paul, which talks about his own weakness and the strength of Christ in him. This idea is repeated many times in the Course, and is but another reminder that we get everything upside down. Somehow we feel strength when we hate and fight back, not letting people treat us like doormats, etc., but associate weakness with turning the other cheek.

For you could not control your joyous response to the call of love if you heard it, and the whole world you thought you made would vanish.

The ego in us knows that if we truly get in touch with this call of love, we would let the ego go and the entire world would disappear for us. That is why it sets up one barrier after another, one line of defense after another, so that we never get to what the real problem is. All those barriers are simply different forms of special relationships, different forms of the dream of the body, and these are what the obstacles to peace are about as well.

The Holy Spirit, then, seems to be attacking your fortress, for you would shut out God, and He does not will to be excluded.

This is why the Holy Spirit would be seen as an enemy in the ego thought system. This is certainly why Jesus was seen by many as an enemy during his life, and continues to be perceived as a threat; and above all, that is why the Course would be seen as an enemy, or a false statement, because it is teaching the exact opposite of everything the ego teaches. Here is another very important line:

You have built your whole insane belief system because you think you would be helpless in God's Presence, and you would save yourself from His Love because you think it would crush you into nothingness. You are afraid it would sweep you away from yourself and make you little, because you believe that magnitude lies in defiance, and that attack is grandeur.

That is the fear, and we have built up a whole insane thought system to "protect" ourselves from the only One in the universe who could help us. In the psychology of many people this works either by defiantly acting out, making themselves into something that is powerful, which really is ego grandiosity, or becoming afraid of that "power," denying it and becoming just the opposite: meek and submissive, letting people take advantage of them or walk all over them. Not realizing these two choices are heads and tails of the same coin, people tend to move from one to the other — often helped by many forms of psychotherapy — without realizing that the whole coin is a defense.

You think you have made a world God would destroy; and by loving Him, which you do, you would throw this world away, which you *would*.

The ego's guilt that demands punishment tells us that God will attack us, because we have attacked and separated from Him. Actually, all the current fears of coming cataclysms and the end of the world are nothing more than different manifestations of this basic ego idea that God will destroy us because of what we have done to Him. The biblical story of Noah's Ark reflects this thinking. It is not just in this age, incidentally, that predictions of impending doom and escalating fear have emerged. Even in the time of Jesus people were predicting the end of the world, and such preoccupations in fact have always been with us. Again, the problem is not that God would destroy the world. How can He destroy when He only loves? The end of the world would simply be our letting the world go. Our investment in the world is our investment in guilt, which protects and defends us from love, and when that investment is gone then the purpose of the world is gone as well.

Therefore, you have used the world to cover your love, and the deeper you go into the blackness of the ego's foundation, the closer you come to the Love that is hidden there. *And it is this that frightens you.*

The first part of this sentence is related to the sections on "The Substitute Reality" and "The Two Worlds" in Chapter 18. First, we have made the world and used it as a cover for this Love of God, indicated at the bottom of Chart B, and everything else is superimposed on top of it to "protect" us from it. Those are the shadows of guilt. As we become more deeply immersed and stuck in the ego system, the presence of love becomes more and more unbearable to us. Therefore the ego's fear is of our getting in touch with the memory and Love of God, at which point the fear of death becomes the strongest. But that is the ego's death, not ours. St. Augustine had a wonderful and insightful description when he commented on suddenly being thrown back into darkness whenever he approached the light. He was really expressing this same phenomenon. His understanding would have been different from ours, but his experience of it was very typical.

You can accept insanity because you made it, but you cannot accept love because you did not.

Remember how the Course draws an analogy between ourselves and what we made, and how parents and animals are with their offspring. Whenever we do or make something, we feel a special attachment to it. Therefore, we do not want to let it go because we see what we have made as a part or projection of ourselves. So we cling to the insanity of the ego system because we have made it. And the ego in us cannot accept love or the Christ in us because we did not make that.

You would rather be a slave of the crucifixion than a Son of God in redemption. Your individual death seems more valuable than your living oneness (that is the attraction of death, the third obstacle), **for what is given you is not so dear as what you made.**

An earlier section, "The Two Emotions," says we have but two emotions: One we made and one was given us. This is parallelled here. The emotion we made is fear and the one given us is love, and that is what we are afraid of.

You are more afraid of God than of the ego, and love cannot enter where it is not welcome. But hatred can, for it enters of its own volition and cares not for yours.

This is why the Holy Spirit or Jesus cannot enter into our mind's awareness and take away the problem. We do not want to be aware of Their loving presence, and consequently we shut Them out of awareness. The way that we can discern we do want Them in our lives is through forgiveness, which is what we will come to a little later. The volition of hatred belongs to the ego, which always has an open invitation to hate and a closed door to forgiveness and love.

You must look upon your illusions and not keep them hidden, because they do not rest on their own foundation. In concealment they appear to do so, and thus they seem to be self-sustained.

In other words, we believe our problems are guilt, sin, sickness, deprivation and anger. We all, especially within a psychological framework, are very expert in understanding where these come from. Yet none of them holds true, and none of them is the real foundation. The real foundation is the defense against the fear of love. That is the issue and that is the foundation.

This is the fundamental illusion on which the others rest. For beneath them, and concealed as long as they are hidden, is the loving mind that thought it made them in anger. And the pain in this mind is so apparent, when it is uncovered, that its need of healing cannot be denied. Not all the tricks and games you offer it can heal it, for here is the real crucifixion of God's Son.

The real crucifixion of God's Son is the choice to see ourselves as separate, and as being expressions of the denial of God's Love. That is crucifixion. It is not something that the world does to us. It is something that we do to our mind. Crucifixion in the Course, to repeat it again, except when it is specifically referring to Jesus, is a symbol of the ego. It is a symbol of punishment, vengeance, sacrifice and death.

And yet he is not crucified.

This is because what God creates cannot be changed or destroyed. Therefore, in truth we cannot be crucified. Only in our delusions can we believe that we are, but again the whole thing is made up.

Here is both his pain and his healing, for the Holy Spirit's vision is merciful and His remedy is quick. Do not hide suffering from His sight, but bring it gladly to Him. Lay before His eternal sanity all your hurt, and let Him heal you. Do not leave any spot of pain hidden from His Light, and search your mind carefully for any thoughts you may fear to uncover. For He will heal every little thought you have kept to hurt you and cleanse it of its littleness, restoring it to the magnitude of God.

This is a very important paragraph in terms of describing what the Course methodology is. It is really asking and training us, as we work through the text and the workbook, to be increasingly sensitive to all of those thoughts of the ego that cross our mind. All thoughts of hurt, bitterness, anger, unfairness, slights and imposition are only different aspects of seeing ourselves as a victim. Once aware of these thoughts we can bring them to the Holy Spirit or Jesus, and ask Their help that we look at the situation differently. Deep within our mind is our pain because of the wrong choices we have made, and yet that is where the healing is too, because we can change our mind. The important phrase, "Do not leave any spot of pain hidden from His Light," is reiterated at the very end of the text, the journey's close, when Jesus says, "and not one spot of darkness still remains to hide the face of Christ from anyone."

Beneath all the grandiosity you hold so dear is your real call for help. For you call for love to your Father as your Father calls you to Himself. In that place which you have hidden, you will only to unite with the Father, in loving remembrance of Him.

In Chapter 21, the section "The Forgotten Song" uses the analogy of Heaven's song that the Son sings to the Father, and the Father sings to the Son. Hearing those "wonderful sounds" is what the ego is most afraid of, and that is why it sets up cacophonous shrieking whose purpose is to camouflage the loving sounds of Heaven.

You will find this place of truth as you see it in your brothers, for though they may deceive themselves, like you they long for the grandeur that is in them. And perceiving it you will welcome it, and it will be yours. For grandeur is the right of God's Son, and no illusions can satisfy him or save him from what he is. Only his love is real, and he will be content only with his reality.

Here again the Course shifts from this wonderful cosmic view of the world being a defense against God, to very specific and practical suggestions. If we really want to find this place of truth, we must forgive. And even if others are deceiving themselves, pretending they are egos by attacking or seeing themselves as attacked, then that attack nonetheless remains a call for help. Often the Course juxtaposes the words grandeur and grandiosity: grandeur is of spirit and grandiosity is of the ego.

Save him from his illusions that you may accept the magnitude of your Father in peace and joy. But exempt no one from your love, or you will be hiding a dark place in your mind where the Holy Spirit is not welcome.

If we attack or hate anyone we are protecting a spot of darkness in our mind, a place of guilt. This says to the Holy Spirit, "You will not enter." This means we are not turning our minds over to Him but rather are listening to the ego by projecting our guilt onto others by attacking them. And that solidifies in our mind the reality of that spot of darkness or guilt, making it real, and at that point love is totally obscured.

And thus you will exempt yourself from His healing power, for by not offering total love you will not be healed completely.

The vision here is that every single last aspect of guilt, every final defense against love, must be brought into awareness, turned over to the Holy Spirit, and let go of completely. Otherwise one cannot offer total love and be healed totally.

Healing must be as complete as fear, for love cannot enter where there is one spot of fear to mar its welcome.

Obviously this truth is an ideal that the Course is presenting to us. But it is an ideal that teaches us that when we do get annoyed, aggravated, fearful or angry, we should not justify the anger, pretend that it is all right, or rationalize that its expression is healthy and normal, or even the Will of God. Realizing that all these feelings are expressions of our ego, which we do not want, we can then ask for help in changing our minds.

You who prefer separation to sanity cannot obtain it in your right mind.

For the word "separation" in the above sentence we can just as easily substitute the word "specialness," which comes in the next sentence. This chapter is almost a direct precursor to Chapter 15, which is the Course's first discussion of special relationships. Basically this passage is talking about the original separation from God and our fear of Him, which led us to set up a bargain with God to demand His special love. This is expressed in the Judaeo-Christian tradition, for example, in the belief that the Jews were the chosen people of God, or that only baptized Christians were saved and special. This is just another way of saying to God, "Please do not get angry at me because of what I have done." And then we demand special love and attention from God, in exchange for which we do certain things for Him. The insanity of this specialness thinking unfortunately found a home in almost all the theologies of formal religions.

You were at peace until you asked for special favor. And God did not give it for the request was alien to Him, and you could not ask this of a Father Who truly loved His Son.

We demanded God be someone He was not. We demanded God be someone who believed in special love and special hate, trading off His love for sacrifice and suffering, and resorting to vengeance when He did not get His way. Nevertheless, what we really hold against God is that He is only pure Love, and not even all of our insanity can change Him. But we wanted to change Him, and therefore in our insane minds we believed that we had.

Therefore you made of Him an unloving father, demanding of Him what only such a father could give (which is punishment). **And the peace of God's Son was shattered, for he no longer understood his Father. He feared what he had made** (which is a world of victims, attack, pain, and death), **but still more did he fear his real Father, having attacked his own glorious equality with Him.**

Having made ourselves insane, we then proceeded to make God insane. Believing we had attacked Him and our "glorious equality with Him," making up a world to replace His, we then became terrified of His wrathful vengeance. Thus all this fear became a defense against the truth of His Love, which knows no sin or separation.

In peace he needed nothing and asked for

nothing. In war he demanded everything and found nothing.

Peace would be the state of Heaven, our being at one with God. But once we had decided to separate from God, believing we had done something terrible to Him, that set into motion the belief God will attack us back, and that of course is war. These ideas are most powerfully stated in Chapter 23, "The War Against Yourself," in which the section on "The Laws of Chaos" appears, which is the clearest statement of the insane thinking of what we believe we did to God.

For how could the gentleness of love respond to his demands, except by departing in peace and returning to the Father?

This is the ego's fear, for it knows that God's gentle Love means its own undoing. The ego thrives on opposition, on "love" that demands and punishes, and is terrified of a love that does not oppose what it does not recognize as real.

If the Son did not wish to remain in peace, he could not remain at all. For a darkened mind cannot live in the light, and it must seek a place of darkness where it can believe it is where it is not.

That is the world. The place of darkness is the guilt in our mind, which we then project out to make a world of guilt in which we seek to hide. Here again we see the Level One principle of all or nothing, light or darkness.

God did not allow this to happen.

There is a wonderful passage in Chapter 23 which describes this same kind of insanity, and then comes the line: "And God thinks otherwise." It is the idea that we think the illusion real, but God thinks otherwise. God did not allow this to happen; not that He forbade it, He simply did not oppose it. If God had opposed it, He would have made the error real. Thus God simply loved us, and how else could the gentleness of Heaven's Love respond to the Son's demands that it be otherwise? All love does is return to the Father, meaning it remains in our minds, though not in the ego's dream. The ego's fear then is that we would also depart back to the Father, leaving the ego non-existent.

Yet you demanded that it happen and therefore believed that it was so.

That is also very important. The separation never happened in reality, but because we wanted it to happen, we *believed* that it had happened. All of this — this entire ego thought system, this entire world — rests on the simple wish that that is what we wanted, and therefore that is what we experience. Thus have we made the world of separation real in our mind. But God thinks otherwise.

To "single out" is to "make alone," and thus make lonely. (That is what we did in the separation.) **God did not do this to you.**

At the end of the story of Adam and Eve in Genesis, we read that God banishes them from the garden. This is a classic example of projection because it was not God that did this to us, but our own insane thinking.

Could He set you apart, knowing that your peace lies in His Oneness? He denied you only your request for pain, for suffering is not of His creation.

God would not and did not play the "special relationship" game with us. He would not make a bargain, demanding that we suffer and sacrifice, in atonement for our attack on Him. That is all our own idea.

Having given you creation, He could not take it from you. He could but answer your insane request with a sane answer that would abide with you in your insanity.

God's "answer" is usually capitalized in the Course, referring specifically to the Holy Spirit. Here, however, where it is lower case, it refers more specifically to the Holy Spirit's message of forgiveness and love, the principle of the Atonement.

For His answer is the reference point beyond illusions, from which you can look back on them and see them as insane.

The end of Chapter 23 talks about lifting ourselves above the battleground and then looking

203

back on what is below, so from that perspective we are able to see it differently. When we are in the midst of the battleground, believing that we are at war with God and with everyone else, it all seems to be very real, i.e., attack, pain and death appear as real. But when we lift above it we realize the entire thing is made up, and everything on the battleground is a defense against the Love of God. This means that whenever we are tempted to be upset, we should lift ourselves above the situation with the help of the Holy Spirit and look on it as He does. This then becomes the reference point from which we can evaluate it.

But seek this place and you will find it, for Love is in you and will lead you there.

Q: As I think back to the first sentence in this section, where Jesus reminds us that it is crucial that we look upon all our hatred and realize its full extent, I realize that this is really a very grueling process, to say the least. I do not think people want to really look at the hatred within their mind. Even in the Introduction to the text it says that the Course aims "at removing the blocks to the awareness of love's presence," and in the "Principles of Miracles" it says "purification is necessary first." Am I correct in surmising that unless we really do this totally — so that no hatred, guilt or fear remain in our minds — we are not going to accept love in any way shape or form, although we might delude ourselves into thinking it is love?

A: Yes, because our guilt would always demand that we be punished and hated, rather than forgiven and loved. Thus, we have to have our guilt removed first. Actually that is really the Course's answer to the problem of dealing with the final obstacle, "The Fear of God," which we will see when we go into "The Lifting of the Veil." Again, nobody is in touch with that fear of God, with that fear of love, and what removes that final veil is the complete forgiveness of one person whom we have made into the absolute villain of our lives. That is why it is so crucial that we actually look upon the hatred that is in us.

Q: Is it not possible that if we forgive one person, for example, someone whom we have made into the great victimizer in our life, we still could retain some hatred?

A: Yes, but then that would mean that the process of forgiveness regarding that person was not absolutely total. In other words, we forgave and let go of a massive chunk of hatred, but there was still hatred left which means that all the blocks to the awareness of love's presence were not totally let go of.

Q: So is the whole process really monitoring and becoming aware of all of the feelings of hatred and annoyance that come up in us, and then asking the Holy Spirit for help?

A: Yes. This is not a course in doing, it is a course in *un*doing. You do not do anything with love, you do not do anything with the fear of love.

What you do is accept the undoing of all of the defenses against that love. That is what lets go of the fear. We will see that when we discuss "The Lifting of the Veil." This, then, is the whole Course process: looking at and monitoring all those angry, hurt, deprived, unfair and victimized feelings, and remembering that we cannot let go of them without the Holy Spirit's help. This means we must choose that place in our mind where He is, and then look down on the battlefield of our ego system. When we do not do that it is because we are really afraid of the love and the peace that is truly within us. That is always the problem and nothing else.

Lesson 34 in the workbook says "I could see peace instead of this." We can know the Love of God instead of the hatred of the ego. That is the choice we make over and over again in everything. Even if we feel the least bit disquieted we should not justify it by defenses or rationalizations. All that the Course says is that none of these feelings is the problem. Instead we should rise above what we are feeling and look at the fact that we have chosen to be upset, which is a decision to keep the Love of Christ and of God away.

Q: So what we really have to do is fine tune all of our thought processes and senses to what our ego self is doing, or what other egos are doing, and recognize that there is another way of perceiving everything. So unless we become ultra-sensitive to each little thing we are not going to become aware of it, and there will still be those spots of darkness and hatred.

A: Right. It is an ongoing vigilance against all of the things that upset us.

The Fear to Look Within

Let us now turn to the top of page 424 in the text, fifth line down, which is part of another parallel section called "The Fear to Look Within," in Chapter 21. We are not going to do the whole section, but will look on those passages that present the same ideas we have been discussing: Nothing in this world is real, nothing in this world is the problem; it is all a defense we have chosen to keep the truth of the Atonement away from us, since that truth is that nothing in this world is real. Thus we have another opportunity to see the great symphonic structure of the Course, where the same ideas or motifs are introduced again and again, in different ways and contexts, similar to a composer's use of different harmonies and instrumental colorations to develop the symphonic theme.

Loudly the ego tells you not to look inward, for if you do your eyes will light on sin, and God will strike you blind.

Referring to the lower part of the right side of Chart B, we see the fear of God, which reflects the ego's lie that God will destroy us. The ego tells us do not look within, but rather look without. So we look outside ourselves to our body, or someone else's body. These are what the first three obstacles to peace are dealing with: the attraction of guilt, pain and death. The ego says do anything else, but do not look within, because if you do God will destroy you and strike you blind.

This you believe, and so you do not look. Yet this is not the ego's hidden fear, nor yours who serve it. Loudly indeed the ego claims it is; too loudly and too often. For underneath this constant shout and frantic proclamation, the ego is not certain it is so. Beneath your fear to look within because of sin is yet another fear, and one which makes the ego tremble.

The ego tells us that if we look within we will see the blackness of sin. This is parallelled in the opening paragraph in workbook lesson 93, "Light and peace and joy abide in me:"

You think you are the home of evil, darkness and sin. You think if anyone could see the truth about you he would be repelled, recoiling from you as if from a poisonous snake. You think if what is true about you were revealed to you, you would be struck with horror so intense that you would rush to death by your own hand, living on after seeing this being impossible.
These are beliefs so firmly fixed that it is difficult to help you see that they are based on nothing.

This expresses the same idea. We all are so terrified of what we believe to be the horrible truth about ourselves that we continually project this "truth" onto other people, and get upset by everything else around us. And all the while the real truth about us — our innocence — remains obscure. Now we continue on page 424 in the text.

What if you looked within and saw no sin? This "fearful" question is one the ego never asks. And you who ask it now are threatening the ego's whole defensive system too seriously for it to bother to pretend it is your friend.

If we looked within beyond all the darkness of the ego system we would see the sinlessness of God's Son, our true Self, and why we do not look is the one question the ego would never have us ask.

Those who have joined their brothers have detached themselves from their belief that their identity lies in the ego. A holy relationship is one in which you join with what is part of you in truth. And your belief in sin has been already shaken, nor are you now entirely unwilling to look within and see it not.

The viciousness with which the ego strikes back is either directed towards ourselves, in terms of making us physically sick, or psychologically sick such as becoming anxious, depressed or even psychotic; or else the ego becomes vicious in its attack on others. Usually we do both, attack ourselves and attack others in one form or another. We can find all kinds of things to get upset about, and to feel justified in seeing ourselves unfairly treated. All this is a defense against truly being gentle, peaceful and loving within ourselves.

Now let us skip to the end of the section on the top of page 425.

And now the ego *is* afraid. (This is when the ego becomes very vicious.) **Yet what it hears in terror, the other part hears as the sweetest music; the song it longed to hear since first the ego came into your mind.**

The opening section in Chapter 21, "The Forgotten Song," which I already referred to, is the reference here: the song of love that God sings to His Son and His Son sings to Him.

The ego's weakness is its strength. The song of freedom, which sings the praises of another world, brings to it hope of peace. For it remembers Heaven, and now it sees that Heaven has come to earth at last, from which the ego's rule has kept it out so long. Heaven has come because it found a home in your relationship on earth. And earth can hold no longer what has been given Heaven as its own.

Look gently on your brother, and remember the ego's weakness is revealed in both your sight.

The ego's weakness is the simple fact that it does not exist. The whole thing is a house of cards, or a house made of straw. And if we truly want to know that we are children of love and remember Heaven's song, then we must first extend that love to each other. This is still another expression of that basic formula we have already discussed: We see the face of Christ in each other, and then remember God.

What it would keep apart has met and joined (i.e., the love in me joined with the love in you; the attraction of love for love) **and looks upon the ego unafraid.**

Here, as in "The Fear of Redemption," we are asked to look without fear upon the ego so that we can realize that it is nothing.

Little child, innocent of sin, follow in gladness the way to certainty. Be not held back by fear's insane insistence that sureness lies in doubt. This has no meaning. What matters it to you how loudly it is proclaimed?

The basic doubt we all share is the doubt of who we are. The raucous shrieks of the world, at all different levels, affect us because of our basic self-doubt, which the world then seems to uphold.

The senseless is not made meaningful by repetition and by clamor. The quiet way is open. Follow it happily, and question not what must be so.

As we have seen, "The Fear of Redemption" ends in a similar way: "But seek this place and you will find it, for Love is in you and will lead you there."

Looking Within

Another section which parallels many of the ideas that we will talk about in the final obstacle is "Looking Within" in Chapter 12. In this section Jesus speaks quite directly of himself and of our ability to see him as we forgive. Keep in mind that the principal idea of these passages we are considering is our fear of looking within, not really because of what the ego tells us but because of what it does not tell us. We begin at the top of page 216.

You are afraid of me because you looked within and are afraid of what you saw.

We are afraid of Jesus because we made him into a symbol of sacrifice and suffering and, above all, of our own sin. That is what the ego made of him so that we could not see him as he really is, which would be the mirror of our innocence and sinlessness. We looked within ourselves and saw the blackness of guilt (this section talks a great deal about guilt) and, since guilt demands punishment, we believe Jesus would punish us for our sins.

Yet you could not have seen reality, for the reality of your mind is the loveliest of God's creations. (This reality is love.) **Coming only from God, its power and grandeur could only bring you peace** *if you really looked upon it.*

213

Our belief in this delusion revolves around our terror to really look on the truth in us. Instead, we choose to look on the illusions of fear, pain, terror and death, and then we defend ourselves against these illusions. That is what the Course is saying is so ludicrous. We fight to protect ourselves against something that is not there; we made the whole thing up.

If you are afraid, it is because you saw something that is not there (separation, sin, guilt, etc.). **Yet in that same place** (within our mind) **you could have looked upon me and all your brothers, in the perfect safety of the Mind which created us. For we are there in the peace of the Father, Who wills to extend His peace through you.** (Skip down a paragraph.)

When you look within and see me, it will be because you have decided to manifest truth.

In many "New Age" paths the idea is found that we manifest what we want. Here the Course is saying that once we let go of all illusions and the dictates of our ego self, all that we will naturally manifest or reflect is truth, which is the Love of God and Jesus. The Course would teach that it makes no sense to attempt to manifest what we need, for we cannot ever know what we need, although the ego thinks it knows. Without knowing the problem how can we know the solution? Thus the Course should never be misinterpreted to mean manifesting material things in the world. In the real world all that we can manifest is truth, which comes from that place within our minds where the Love of God dwells.

And as you manifest it you will see it both without and within.

Clearly, if we look within and see only the innocence and Love of Christ, then everything we behold outside will mirror what has been beheld within.

Let us skip to the last paragraph at the end of this section, on page 217, where Jesus speaks of how we extend his love by looking on others as he does, without judgment.

When you are tempted to yield to the desire for death (when we feel ourselves being attracted to death as the answer to our problems of pain), *remember that I did not die.*

There is a wonderful poem that Helen had taken down called "Easter," whose opening lines state the same idea:

**I did not die. In rising up I did
But stay the same.**

One of the major corrections that the Course makes to traditional Christian thinking is that Jesus did not truly die on the cross (in fact no one truly dies). Death, as we have seen, is merely a belief in the ego mind that logically follows from our belief in the reality of sin and guilt. Death can only occur in our mind. The body neither lives nor dies; it simply acts out the projections of the mind. The "tragic" result of the Christian belief that Jesus did die was the erection of a theology of crucifixion that established sin, sacrifice and punishment as reality, not to mention a vengeful God who set up this insane plan of salvation.

You will realize that this is true when you look within and *see* me.

This does not mean we will see Jesus perceptually. The text is talking about seeing him, as Hamlet says, "in our mind's eye," which comes about by an attitude born of complete forgiveness. We cannot look within and see Jesus — the great symbol of love and forgiveness in this world — if there is hatred in our heart. The pure light that he is will be marred and obscured by the darkness of our guilt.

Would I have overcome death for myself alone? And would eternal life have been given me of the Father unless He had also given it to you?

In other words, Jesus did not receive anything that we do not have. God did not give him any special gifts, any special graces. This too is a correction for the traditional Christian view that Jesus was different from everyone else. He is telling us that whatever the Father gave him was given to all of us: the gift of eternal life bestowed on us in our creation.

When you learn to make me manifest (and we make him manifest through our forgiveness of each other), **you will never see death.**

Learning to make Jesus manifest comes through forgiveness, because he stands within our holy relationships; undoing separation through forgiveness, we let go of all the guilt in our mind, producing a shift in consciousness the Course refers to as the real world. If there is no guilt there cannot be the belief in death. Death came into our minds through our guilt, because the ego made the world as an opposite to Heaven and eternal life. The ego also made the body that had to be punished and killed in order to atone for its sins. So without guilt in our minds, through the process of forgiveness, we will never believe in death, and through the transformation in consciousness to the real world we will understand that death is only an illusion.

For you will have looked upon the deathless in yourself (the innocence of God's Son), **and you will see only the eternal as you look out upon a world that cannot die.**

In this one paragraph Jesus is uniting the third and fourth obstacles, undoing the attraction and desire for death by explaining to us how we can make him manifest in our minds and hearts through forgiveness of each other.

The Closing of the Gap

Let us now turn to the beginning of Chapter 29. Even though this section, "The Closing of the Gap," comes much later than the Obstacles to Peace, it parallels the final obstacle. "Gap" is a word that is used in the later chapters of the Course to connote separation. Many of these sections discuss sickness and the seeds of sickness that occur in the gap: the belief in separation that is in our mind. Basically the "closing of the gap" is the undoing of the belief in separation.

There is no time, no place, no state where God is absent. There is nothing to be feared.

This denies the entire ego system. Only if God were absent — if there were a gap, if there were separation — would fear be justified. As we have seen many times, the sin of separation leads to guilt, which demands our punishment by a God who deserves to be feared.

There is no way in which a gap could be conceived of in the Wholeness that is His. The compromise the least and the littlest gap would represent in His eternal Love is quite impossible.

Those words, "the least and the littlest," had tremendous meaning for Helen in terms of her own family life. It was Jesus' reminder of her need to forgive, and that no belief in the "least

218

and the littlest" can ever be justified. That phrase is also referred to in Helen's poem "Deliverance."

For it would mean His Love could harbor just a hint of hate, His gentleness turn sometimes to attack, and His eternal patience sometimes fail. All this do you believe, when you perceive a gap between your brother and yourself.

If we see someone as separate from ourselves, having separate interests from our own — some aspect of our investment in specialness — then we are compromising our awareness of God's Love. As the Course reflects in many places, compromise is one of the ego's major tactics in keeping this world of separation intact. Practically all thought systems in this world, including most spiritual and religious systems, effect some kind of compromise between truth and illusion, reality and illusion, spirit and the body.

How could you trust Him, then? For He must be deceptive in His Love.

This again is the idea, presented so forcefully in "The Laws of Chaos," that we set up a God who is as deceptive, insane and fearful as we are.

Be wary, then; let Him not come too close, and leave a gap between you and His Love, through which you can escape if there be need for you to flee.

The ego has told us that God is an enemy and

we must keep Him away. As we have seen reflected at the bottom of the right-hand box in
Chart B, that fear is the second line of defense
against the ego's first line of defense, which is
that we have to keep God away because He is
Love. We keep God separate from us by keeping
His Son separate from us. Thus the Christ becomes split and we see gaps between us and everyone else, gaps between our self and our Self
because we believe our body is real. Again, the
gap is what keeps God away, which the text now
discusses.

Here is the fear of God most plainly seen.

We can see the Course moving back and forth
between this ontological view of our relationship
with God and the specific ways that we live with
each other.

**For love *is* treacherous to those who fear, since
fear and hate can never be apart. No one who
hates but is afraid of love, and therefore must he
be afraid of God.**

We will see that same idea very powerfully expressed in "The Lifting of the Veil" — i.e., "You
are afraid of God *because* you fear your brother."
In other words, we hate because we have chosen
to hate — to see separation outside — because we
are afraid of the unity of the love that is within us.

Certain it is he knows not what love means (anyone who chooses hate). **He fears to love and loves**

to hate, and so he thinks that love is fearful; hate is love. This is the consequence the little gap must bring to those who cherish it, and think that it is their salvation and their hope.

The fear of God! The greatest obstacle that peace must flow across has not yet gone. The rest are past, but this one still remains to block your path, and make the way to light seem dark and fearful, perilous and bleak. You had decided that your brother is your enemy. Sometimes a friend, perhaps, provided that your separate interests made your friendship possible a little while.

Obviously that is a direct reference back to Chapter 19. Jesus is giving us the benefit of the doubt here that we have gone through the first three obstacles. Just as in "The Last Unanswered Question" in Chapter 21, it is the last question that we have trouble with: "And do I want to see what I denied *because* it is the truth?" As Jesus says: "You may have already answered the first three questions, but not yet the last. For this one still seems fearful, and unlike the others." Since we have chosen to deny the truth in us, which is love, a decision we have made, we are reminded again that we can now change our mind about it. But that requires that we do not bring different elements of hate into our holy relationships and deem them tolerable.

But not without a gap between you, lest he turn again into an enemy. A cautious friendship, limited in scope and carefully restricted in amount, became the treaty you had made with him.

We always have to keep the other person away from us, because ultimately we want to keep God away from us. In other words, there is an unconscious bargain that we make with each other. Very often good friends or lovers make an unconscious bargain that they are going to act out against each other. For example, we will do little things that will annoy the other person, and in a sense that becomes expected and is built into the relationship, very much like a treaty. We do not usually break the overall relationship, but there are lots of little digs that we do. They become expected, if not demanded, because they prove we are separate. Thus, a little bit of hate is made real, which of course makes the whole ego system real.

You shared a qualified entente, in which a clause of separation was a point on which you both agreed to keep intact. And violating this was thought to be a breach of treaty not to be allowed.

That is the gap that we have placed between ourselves and each other, and have promised to uphold. Let us skip now to the end of the section, beginning seven lines from the bottom of page 564. This will also be a nice lead-in to "The Lifting of the Veil."

And there are overtones of seeming fear around the happy message, "God is Love."

That again is what the ego is always telling us, and is the very kernal of the ego's fear: God is

Love. There is an important and powerful line, bottom of page 471, that says: "Forgive your Father it was not His Will that you be crucified." What the ego holds against God is that it was not His Will to punish or crucify us. His loving Will is simply perfect happiness for us. And that is what we hold against God and Jesus and, in fact, still hold against Jesus.

Yet all that happens when the gap is gone is peace eternal. Nothing more than that, and nothing less.

Remember that the ego tells us that if we let go of the gap and forgive another person, letting go of our dreams of victimization and special relationships, then what is left is our terror of God's wrathful vengeance. Jesus is telling us here that all that happens when the gap is gone is peace eternal. Therefore, we do not have to do anything with the fear of God, nor even confront our terror of God. All we do is let go of the barriers to this fear, which are the layers of defense we have seen in the right-hand box in Chart B; and when all that remains is the fear of God, that too will disappear because there is nothing left to uphold it. The whole dream then disappears and "all that happens . . . is peace eternal."

Without the fear of God, what could induce you to abandon Him? What toys or trinkets in the gap could serve to hold you back an instant from His Love? Would you allow the body to say "no" to Heaven's calling, were you not afraid to find a

loss of self in finding God? Yet can your self be lost by being found?

This fear of losing our self is why we choose to hold onto the ego's "toys and trinkets," and to the little expressions of sin that we manifest in our relationships. This loss is what the ego tells us is inevitable when we forgive and find God, and it has been one of the major criticisms of mysticism. Mystics have often been accused of teaching the annihilation of the self. If the mystical literature is misread it does seem like that is what is taught, just as if the Course is misread.

However, the self is not annihilated; the ego self simply disappears. The loss of self that we are terrified of is what we believe will be the dissolution of the body, or loss of ego self-identification, and this comes from our equating the ego with the body, or the ego with our self. But that personal self-identification is one of guilt, attack, separation, depression, sickness, loss and death, and it is only *that* self that goes. What remains is the right-minded self that constitutes our living in the real world. This state is beautifully described, for example, in "The Forgiven World" in Chapter 17, and "Where Sin Has Left" in Chapter 26.

Q: Does that mean since we do not know what the spiritual Self is, we first have to let go of the ego self that we do identify with?

A: Yes. But the position of the world would be that there is no spiritual Self.

Q: Does that then leave such a person in the position that there is absolutely nothing but a vacuum?

A: Right. And that is what psychoanalysts have always taught psychosis is, a loss of ego self-identity, which is believed to be our only identity. Therefore, what psychoanalysts say is true within their thought system. If you define mysticism as an experience of oneness with God or creation, and your thought system denies anything that is not material, as does psychoanalysis, then what you are talking about is a psychosis. Actually Franz Alexander, one of the more famous psychoanalysts, wrote a paper on the mystical experience of Buddhism being a narcissistic regression to the infant nursing at the mother's breast.

Once you believe that the material world is all there is, you must accept Alexander's conclusion. You must teach that anything that unites you with a non-material state must be psychotic because that is what your thought system demands. The premises of a thought system dictate what the conclusions must be. The goal of the Course is not the dissolution of the separated self, but only the wrong-minded aspect of this ego self. As the text says on page 322: "Fear not that you will be abruptly lifted up and hurled into reality." The goal of the Course is the transformation of the ego self and the attainment of the real world, not the transcendence of the self and return to Heaven. Actually you could even spell the "self" at the end of the section with a capital "S". This same point is made in some beautiful passages in "The Lifting of the Veil," to which we now return.

The Lifting of the Veil (cont.)

This section is the culmination of the four obstacles. Almost this entire section deals with the forgiveness that Jesus asks us to offer each other, for this is the way that we pass through this final terrifying veil. As we have already seen, the Course does not ask us to confront the fear of God and all its terror. What it is talking about is that we have to confront all the insane defenses we placed between ourselves and God, which really means that *all* we have to do is forgive those specific people with whom we walk this journey. The metaphor used here is the image of a journey.

Forget not that you came this far together, you and your brother. And it was surely not the ego that led you here.

Obviously it is not the ego that would lead us before this final veil. And the final veil consists of truly forgiving one other person, although for many of us it may not be just one particular person, but a number of people who are difficult lessons for us.

Q: Can you clarify what you meant by saying that we do not face the fear of God directly, but that we only have to face the difficult and painful relationships in our life?

A: Basically what I am talking about is the process

that you do not have to meditate on God and try
to surround yourself or Him with light, or try not
to see Him as fearful but as loving. However,
what we are urged to do as we meditate is to
bring the thought of a particular person that we ✗
hold the most grievances against to the Holy
Spirit. It is in the process of forgiving that person
that the fear of God is undone. Ultimately it is the
hatred of another that holds in place the attraction
of the body, guilt, pain and death, and the fear of
God. When we truly forgive someone else everything else disappears.

In other words, you do not have to meditate on ✗
the last obstacle to peace in terms of trying to picture God differently. If you picture your brother
differently the guilt is undone, which then re-
leases God from that projection of fear. That is
what the very specific and unique process of the
Course consists of, and that is why this final section of "The Obstacles to Peace" is all about forgiveness. It is our hatred and fear of our brother
that leads us to be afraid of God. And when we
let go of that hatred of someone else the guilt
goes, which means the projection of guilt goes,
which means we no longer demand that God
punish us.

Q: Later on this section talks about wandering
away, only to come back again. What does this
mean?

A: Specifically that refers to a relationship that is
crucial to our own spiritual path; a relationship
that will bring out all of that hidden guilt and ha-

tred. And if we do not choose to really forgive then we wander off, only to come this way again. So if we cannot work through difficult relationships and have them healed by forgiveness, then we must wander off only to return to this problem at some later time. This is what the journey is all about. Again, it is not the ego that would lead us to this spot when we can finally make that decision to truly forgive.

No obstacle to peace can be surmounted through its help (i.e., the ego's help). **It does not open up its secrets, and bid you look on them and go beyond them.**

It is not the ego that would tell us to look at what is really happening, or to look at what the ego thought system really is. Obviously that is not what the ego does. Its whole purpose is to obscure its thought system so that we do not look at what it is.

It would not have you see its weakness, and learn it has no power to keep you from the truth.

The ego does not want us to look within. It does not want us to see what its system is all about. Remember the movie "The Wizard of Oz" where the wizard is portrayed as this great and powerful person. However, it ends up that he is an ordinary man sitting in front of a huge amplifier, booming out a voice that frightens people. That is what the ego is. Elsewhere the text talks about the ego as a "frightened mouse that roars at the universe." The ego never wants us to look at that truth about itself. It tells us all about the terrible things that are happening to us, and that things have to be different in the world so that we can feel better. It makes all the problems outside of us seem real.

The Guide Who brought you here (the Holy Spirit) **remains with you, and when you raise your eyes you will be ready to look on terror with no fear at all. But first, lift up your eyes and look on one another in innocence born of complete forgiveness of each other's illusions, and through the eyes of faith that sees them not.**

Now when we have truly forgiven each other we can look on the images we have made of each other and of God, and realize that all of them are really nothing; we can finally look on terror and realize there is no terror. However, if we do not forgive completely, then we are retaining guilt, which demands punishment, and then God will be seen as frightening because we are thinking exactly as the ego wants us to do. However, this passage should not be taken to imply that both people in a relationship have to do this together, although it could be misconstrued that way. It is always nice when that happens. However, if that were the case it would mean that my forgiveness would depend on your forgiveness of me, which only sets up a condition where I must feel victimized by your choice not to forgive me. All that is necessary for my salvation is for me to forgive you totally, regardless of your choices, and then that forgiveness is extended by the Holy Spirit

through me to you, where it is held until the time
you can accept it. Another way to understand
why forgiveness must work that way is to think of
Jesus. He obviously forgave the world, which just
as obviously did not forgive him. Yet I doubt if
anyone would maintain that his salvation was in-
complete because of the world's unforgiveness.

**No one can look upon the fear of God unterri-
fied, unless he has accepted the Atonement and
learned illusions are not real.**

Accepting the Atonement can be defined as denying the reality of the separation and all that
seemed to follow from it. The big illusion of the
world is that the separation is real, therefore sin,
guilt and fear seem real. When I truly join with
you through complete forgiveness, and undo all
of my ego barriers to that experience of unity with
you, then I have accepted the Atonement for myself; I have denied the reality of the world's illusions, including the illusion of the final obstacle,
that God is to be feared. Thus the whole ego system goes as one.

That unity of the ego system, along with the
unity of salvation, is the consistent focus of the
Course, and points up why these obstacles are
such an important part of the text. They make so
very clear that the whole process of salvation can
be boiled down to one basic idea: forgiveness. In
that forgiveness — seeing the face of Christ in another — is returned to us the memory of God, the
Course's formula of salvation we have discussed
before. To see the face of Christ in our brother or

sister is to look at that person through the eyes of —
total forgiveness, and to recognize the innocence
and oneness with that person. At that point everything on the right-hand side of Chart B disappears: the dreams of victimhood disappear, the
fear of God disappears, and all that is left is the
memory of God dawning in our mind.

**No one can stand before this obstacle alone, for
he could not have reached this far unless his
brother walked beside him.**

This is talking about our standing at the journey's end. We have worked through many of our
grievances, and now we are ready to let go of that
one big grievance that we hold. Again, the
Course is not really talking about a specific thing;
it is reflecting the culmination of a process. This is
another way of saying that the Course's path of
redemption, or salvation, lies through changing a
"special relationship" into a "holy one." As it
says in the "I Need Do Nothing" section of Chapter 18, there are other paths that teach different
ways, such as ones that emphasize long periods
of contemplation or meditation. But this is not the
Course's way.

And no one would dare to look on it (the final
obstacle, "The Fear of God") **without complete
forgiveness of his brother in his heart. Stand you
here a while and tremble not. You will be ready.**

Early in the text, repeated also in the manual,
the Course says that readiness does not mean

mastery. One of the ego's ways to trap us is to have us believe that we must be perfect. But what the Course is telling us is that we can be ready to forgive, we can be ready to take the next steps in our path, without being perfect, without having mastered forgiveness. The Course is implying here that practically no one feels fully capable of the forgiveness or the change of mind that is being talked about here. Yet Jesus is saying that we do not have to be concerned about this: we will be ready, because we are already ready.

One of my favorite lines in this section is: "Together we will disappear into the Presence beyond the veil." In other words, when we join with Jesus along with our brother or sister, our separated egos disappear. The veil would be like a gossamer screen we just pass through. But until that point is reached, the darkness in our mind is projected out and then onto an image of a fiendish God who would destroy us. Yet when total forgiveness is in our hearts the nightmare disappears. But Jesus is telling us to stand here a while without trembling. In one sense the statement is metaphoric, in terms of standing in front of a veil, but it expresses that this is not something we just plunge into.

Total forgiveness is the most difficult thing in the world and it needs a lot of preparation. In fact, at the end of Chapter 1 Jesus says, "This is a course in mind training," and he goes on to say that we must study these earlier sections in order to prepare for the later sections. Otherwise, he cautions, "awe will be confused with fear, and the experience will be more traumatic than beatific." In terms of the Course process, therefore, we need preparation to look on the fear of God and pass through that final veil. And that preparation comes about by a step by step process that the Holy Spirit leads us through, learning to forgive more and more.

Q: Is the word "veil" here also a metaphor?

A: Yes, in Judaism the "holy of holies" was the innermost sanctuary, which is where the presence of God was. It was deemed the most holy place in the world by the Jewish people, and there was a veil in front of it, through which only the High Priest could pass. Matthew's gospel says that at the moment Jesus died, "the veil was rent," which can be understood spiritually to mean the last barrier, the last obstacle between ourselves and God, was removed. So the use of the "veil" definitely has a Judaeo-Christian reference.

Let us join together in a holy instant, here in this place where the purpose, given in a holy instant, has led you.

The holy instant is that instant of true joining with another, when, as the workbook says, "We let miracles replace all grievances." Jesus is asking us to join with him because we cannot do this without his help.

And let us join in faith that He Who brought us here together will offer you the innocence you need, and that you will accept it for my love and His.

That, of course, is the Holy Spirit, who was Jesus' Teacher and Guide, as he explains early in the text. The Holy Spirit then becomes our Guide as well.

Nor is it possible to look on this too soon. This is the place to which everyone must come when he is ready. Once he has found his brother he *is* ready. Yet merely to reach the place is not enough. A journey without a purpose is still meaningless, and even when it is over it seems to make no sense.

So it is not enough just to be with a person in a relationship. We must also recognize what the purpose is: forgiveness. For example, let us say two people spend fifty years living together and finally get to the end of that particular journey. If they do not recognize what the purpose of their life was, then it would seem as if it were senseless. It is only when we realize that this was a lesson in joining, that there are no separate interests and no grievances that are justified, that the whole journey and relationship makes sense.

How can you know that it is over unless you realize its purpose is accomplished? Here, with the journey's end before you, you *see* its purpose.

Before we can realize the journey's purpose is accomplished we have to identify with the purpose. This does not necessarily mean intellectually, but certainly we have to identify with the meaning of it, which means that we truly join with another and let go of all the barriers that kept us apart. The purpose that we now understand is to pass through that veil, that final obstacle. The purpose of being with this person was to truly forgive, and that is what enables us to pass through that final veil.

Here is that wonderful line:

And it is here you choose whether to look upon it or wander on, only to return and make the choice again.

While it is not necessary to understand this line as a confirmation of a belief in past lives or reincarnation, I certainly think that is what it is talking about, although one could also choose to understand it as referring to an individual lifetime. If you are with a person with whom you have journeyed many years, and there is a point beyond which you will not go, i.e., there are some things you will not forgive in that person, then you stand before that veil, hearing the ego words that say, "Do not pass beyond this veil because if you do you will be destroyed." And if you choose to hear that message, it will become experienced in consciousness as "I will not forgive"; or "After what that person did to me, I cannot possibly forgive." We do not experience what the real ego message is: "Choose anger so you will not know love." And if we make that choice, then we do wander off only to return and make the choice again.

The final section of the text is "Choose Once Again." We are always given another chance to make a different choice. As a final reminder, that section states: "Trials are but lessons that you failed to learn presented once again, so where you made a faulty choice before you now can make a better one. . . ." This is basically saying to us that if we forgive whomever we have to forgive, the lessons or trials will not recur again. As difficult and as painful as that choice seems, we are much better off doing it now. If we choose not to forgive, we are choosing to make real our beliefs in sin, the fear of God, the fear of each other, and in the justification of attack, all of which only make it more difficult later on to forgive. That is why some metaphysical systems teach that suicide is a setback in terms of one's overall progress; it reinforces our belief in the reality of the body, the world, and the pain of this world, which merely reinforces our belief that the ego is real.

Therefore, Jesus is encouraging us to look at those relationships that are really difficult, or those situations that seem to bring up so much discomfort in us, and work them through with his help; otherwise we will only have to deal with them again. And if we choose to wander off — not to heal this relationship — we are really making the choice again to keep the Love of God away from us. The ego's mechanism of repression or denial is so powerful that we will not be aware that that is what we are doing. We will think we are justified in our anger with this person, whatever the situation, and not be aware that what we are really doing is keeping who we truly are away from us, and keeping God away from us as well.

To look upon the fear of God does need some preparation.

The Course is not advocating that we jump right into this. That is why I mentioned earlier the mind training talked about at the end of Chapter 1. Remember that we are talking about letting go of tremendous feelings of guilt and terror, and all of these become encapsulated in the grievances that we hold against each other. And we do not let that go easily. One of the important psychological principles is that we do not take people's defenses away from them. Jesus upholds that principle in the earlier parts of the Course when he says that he cannot take our fear away from us. As we saw earlier, the Holy Spirit does not take our hatred away from us either. If we are holding on to it, it is because we are still afraid of the Love of God that lies beyond the hatred, and the Holy Spirit waits patiently until we are prepared to approach it.

Only the sane can look on stark insanity and raving madness with pity and compassion, but not with fear.

What makes us sane is to allow the undoing of the insane thinking of the ego.

For only if they share in it does it seem fearful (only if we share in the insanity or the madness of the world does all of it seem real and therefore to be feared), **and you do share in it until you look upon your brother with perfect faith and love and tenderness.**

Certainly this is one of the clearest statements in the Course, reminding us again that if we truly want to remember our Father we must share in practicing Jesus' teaching of total forgiveness of everyone. And if we do not, then the fear of God and of the world will become very real to us.

Before complete forgiveness you still stand unforgiving.

The scene here is that we are standing terrified before this veil of total forgiveness, and so we "still stand unforgiving"; we are still holding onto certain grievances. Complete forgiveness is what enables us to move beyond that final veil. Again, we do not have to confront the terror of God, because that is not the problem, nor is that what our experience is. This next line is very important.

You are afraid of God *because* you fear your brother.

Now the converse of this statement is also true on an unconscious level, in terms of how the process began. We became afraid of God when we attempted in the separation to usurp His role as Creator and Source of all being. Next we repressed and denied that fear, and then proceeded to erect the massive ego thought system, this dream of victimization depicted in the right-hand box in Chart B. Within that dream we learned to fear each other. It is the same dynamic that occurs in special relationships. Our first attempt at a special relationship was with God. Furthermore, when we denied our "war" with God, we chose to have special relationships with everyone else. So that the converse is true in terms of its origin. But in terms of the undoing of the problem, the reverse is true: What keeps the fear of God intact is our fear of our brother, which gets us into our specific dreams of victimization, of the body, and special relationships.

Those you do not forgive you fear.

This is in answer to someone who says, "I am not afraid of this person." Jesus is telling us here that if we do not forgive that person we must fear him, because our lack of forgiveness is an attack on him and on ourself. If we attack that person, then our ego will demand that we be attacked in return, and we will fear that attack. It is our fear of someone else that reinforces our fear of God because that is the expression of the principle, "Defenses do what they would defend." The purpose of a defense is to protect us from fear, but it merely reinforces fear. So the purpose of the defenses of attacking and fearing our brother is to protect us from the fear of God, or so the ego tells us; but of course that merely strengthens the fear. Once again, those whom we do not forgive we must fear.

Q: Why do most people not experience directly that if they do not forgive someone they are really fearful of them?

A: The ultimate reason why we do not is that it would give the ego away.

Q: Something I have been aware of since working with the Course is that you do start to become aware of all this. I am starting to see that when I am angry I am also afraid of that person. I think that is also a process, and as you begin to take the ultimate truths and apply them on an individual level, you begin to see that it is not even unconscious; it is really conscious and you can feel this fear welling up.

A: Workbook lesson 136, "Sickness is a defense against the truth," talks about how all decisions to be sick, and this would include decisions to be fearful and angry, are conscious. There is then a split second when we push these decisions into the unconscious. This is in keeping with Freud's famous dictum that the purpose of psychoanalysis was to make the unconscious conscious. The Course is actually saying the same thing; the process is a little different but the idea is the same. As you work with these ideas more and more you realize if you are angry you *must* be afraid. Similarly, if you are fearful then you must be angry. The ego system is one complete package.

Q: Is there anywhere in the psychological literature outside the Course which states that?

A: Not that I am aware of. The thinking of the psychological community, many of whom are turning more and more to spirituality in one form or another, would reject the Course because the other forms of spirituality would allow them to compromise in order to have a little bit of truth and a little bit of illusion. The Course process does not allow for that, as it says that everything in the world is really just a defense against God.

Q: What was Freud's understanding of guilt, attack, fear and projection?

A: Freud never said that when you attack someone you would feel guilty in return. Because of his Victorian background, he was not big on expressing anger. I have never seen anywhere in the psychological literature that when you attack someone you will feel guilty, unless you are talking about people who are already coming from a spiritual point of view. Yet that is why the Course is so emphatic that anger is never justified, because anger has always been taught as an inherent part of being human, part of being a person. To say that anger is never justified would be heard by most psychologists as a denial of who you are, and they would say it is possible to attack without feeling guilty.

I think one of the clearest examples of that kind of thinking would be Scott Peck's book, *People of the Lie*, where he has constructed a psychological system, which he then theologizes, in which it is healthy to see evil in another person and, moreover, that such perception has nothing to do with the projections of the analyst. Furthermore, that is why the Course talks so much about the idea that if you give something you receive it; if you give anger then you are going to get it back.

Again, the idea that the entire ego system is a defense against the Love of God does not appear anywhere but in the Course. What makes the

Course such a unique and remarkable document, the perfect spiritual tool for our age, is its use of psychology integrated with a very high level of spirituality. Because we in the 20th century are very much students of psychology, we need a spirituality that draws upon psychology to help us understand the very foundation of the ego system. As an example of this integration, let us review a part of workbook lesson 136 that I mentioned before. The passage is on page 250, in the middle of the fourth paragraph.

All this cannot be done unconsciously. (This is discussing the choices that we make.) **But afterwards, your plan requires that you must forget you made it, so it seems to be external to your own intent; a happening beyond your state of mind, an outcome with a real effect on you, instead of one effected by yourself.**
It is this quick forgetting of the part you play in making your "reality" that makes defenses seem to be beyond your own control.

It is our experience that everything happens *to* us, that we are innocent victims of the world. Furthermore, we do not make the connection that would help us understand that those we hold grievances against are people whom we fear. The whole thing, again, is a massive defensive system against the Love of God. We return now to where we left off at the end of the fourth paragraph on page 393 in the text.

And no one reaches love with fear beside him.

"Perfect love casts out fear," as John's first epistle taught. The ego knows that if we allow love in our heart then there is no place for fear, or the ego. But it also works the other way around, in that fear obscures perfect love. (This, incidentally, is not mentioned in John's letter.) So if we choose fear, which comes with choosing grievances and unforgiveness, then we are also choosing above all to keep love away. We can say then that everything here is intention, choice and a decision: a choice to be upset, angry, disappointed, disillusioned, and to feel victimized; a choice to keep the Love of God away, even though the situation does not appear that way.

This brother who stands beside you still seems to be a stranger.

This is a use of the word "stranger" that is directly based on the parable of "The Last Judgment" in Matthew 25, where Jesus says: "I was a stranger and you took me in." On page 396 in the text, the fourth line from the bottom, written on Palm Sunday, Jesus says:

I was a stranger and you took me in, not knowing who I was. Yet for your gift of lilies you will know. In your forgiveness of this stranger, alien to you and yet your ancient Friend ("ancient Friend" capitalized refers to Christ), **lies his release and your redemption with him.**

This is one of the few places in the text, incidentally, where Helen had felt very moved and experienced a deep sense of gratitude in taking the

Course down. The gift of lilies is the Course's symbol of forgiveness, especially relevant at Eastertime because that is the Easter flower. Jesus is saying that when we chose to join with our brother we were taking him in. But at the moment that we began the relationship we did not realize that was what we were doing. Yet through the forgiveness of the special relationship, which then becomes a holy relationship, we will then know who Jesus really is.

Let us return again to the bottom of page 393.

You do not know him, and your interpretation of him is very fearful.

This is our opportunity truly to let go of the ego, here in this relationship with this special person, and we are still finding it difficult to choose forgiveness and the holy relationship. Therefore that person is a stranger to us and we do not recognize that person as our brother or sister in Christ. We do not see the face of Christ because we are still obscuring it with our anger and our grievances. And our interpretation is fearful because we are still attacking.

And you attack him still, to keep what seems to be yourself unharmed.

This is the ego's way to protect ourselves. What seems to be ourselves is the ego, and the ego teaches us by attacking somebody else we are off the hook, we are protected. It is as if there is a barrier built around us and it is a barrier of hatred. That is the gap that we talked about earlier.

Yet in his hands is your salvation.

That does not mean that that person has special powers. It does not mean that that person is our savior because of his or her ego. It means that that person is our savior because if we choose to see him or her as our brother or sister then we are saved. And this presupposes no response on the part of the other person. Sometimes the other person could be dead and so would not even be physically present. The person would still be in our mind and that is enough.

You see his madness, which you hate because you share it.

Remember the line in workbook lesson 134 which says that whenever we are tempted to accuse anyone of anything we should stop and ask ourself: "Would I accuse myself of doing this?" Whenever we hate what we see in another person it is only because we do not want to see it in ourselves. If I hate something in you, criticize something in you, judge against something in you, it is only because I first saw it in myself and hate it, even though it may take a different form in me. I see what I judge to be your sin and believe that I share it, and that is what I hate.

And all the pity and forgiveness that would heal it gives way to fear.

Jesus is here using the word "pity" in a positive sense. There are other places in the Course where "pity" would really be synonymous with false

—empathy. Here "pity" expresses more the sense of the other person's pain which we realize is our own; it is a call for the love that we do not feel that we deserve. That is true empathy. And we realize that while we share the same weakness of the ego and fear of God's Love, at the same time we are aware that there is within us both the strength of Christ's Love.

Brother, you need forgiveness of each other, for you will share in madness or in Heaven together. And you will raise your eyes in faith together, or not at all.

There are other places in the Course where we have that same theme: "The ark of peace is entered two by two"; "Salvation is a collaborative venture"; "No one enters Heaven by himself." This is the Course process. The way that we will enter the ark of peace — penetrate beyond this final veil, this final obstacle and simply know God as He is — is through forgiveness of another person. Nevertheless, it does not mean that on the level of form a person walks through the veil with us. It means that within our mind, since minds are joined and there is no one outside anyway, we do not experience that person as separate.

If you see forgiveness any other way, trying to explain what happened to Jesus will be difficult. Practically no one walked through the veil with him, although he brought everyone with him because he knew everyone was joined with him in his mind. The manual says that we were with Jesus when he arose. We were with him because he knew that we were with him. But we choose to remain asleep. Remember if I see madness in you, it is because I see it in myself; if I see Heaven in you, then I see it in myself. And if I see Heaven in myself by having forgiven everything that I believe is of the ego in myself and you, then you are healed as well. This is true even though within the illusion of time there may be a considerable time lapse before you choose to accept it. "Faith," as the Course uses the word, is really not so much faith in God, although it does use it like that occasionally; it is faith in your brother and sister that the light of Christ shines in them despite all of the ego darkness. It does not mean that we deny what the other person has done. It simply means that we look beyond the behavior, seeing it as a call for help, our own included, and that is what we join with.

Beside each of you is one who offers you the chalice of Atonement, for the Holy Spirit is in him.

The chalice of Atonement is a very strong Christian symbol, referring to the chalice of the Last Supper mentioned in the gospels. Jesus is said to have blessed the wine, and passed it around saying that anyone who drinks of this would be saved, since the wine had become identified with his blood. Obviously Jesus is talking about something totally different here. Our brothers and sisters offer us the chalice of Atonement by offering us the opportunity to undo the projections of our ego onto them, and to make another choice.

Would you hold his sins against him, or accept his gift to you? Is this giver of salvation your friend or enemy?

Everything boils down to choice. In the final section of the text, "Choose Once Again," we find the same idea on the bottom of page 619:

> **"Choose once again if you would take your place**
> **among the saviors of the world, or would**
> **remain in hell, and hold your brothers there."**

That is the ultimate expression of what is being talked about here. If I hold your sins against you I am not only reinforcing my sinfulness, I am doing the same for you. We return to "The Lifting of the Veil":

Choose which he is, remembering that you will receive of him according to your choice.

This whole aspect of choosing is absolutely essential to the Course, and while the world presents us with many different choices, in truth there is only one. It is a choice between truth and illusion, sin and forgiveness, the anti-Christ or Christ.

He has in him the power to forgive your sin, as you for him. Neither can give it to himself alone. And yet your savior stands beside each one. Let him be what he is, and seek not to make of love an enemy.

This is harking back to the biblical theme we discussed earlier where Jesus says, "Those whose sins you forgive are forgiven, those whose sins you retain are retained." Obviously, here it is given a totally different meaning. You have the power to forgive my sin because you could deny the seeming fact that we are separate, and I can do the same for you. I cannot forgive my own sins: "Neither can give it to himself alone." If I do it for me, I must do it for you; and vice versa, since we are one and the same.

This bears directly on the importance of that crucial metaphysical premise of the Course that there is no world outside of our mind. Minds are joined, bodies are not joined. You are not separate from me; whatever I see in you, whatever I do to you in my mind or in behavior, is always what I do to myself because it is one and the same. The inner and the outer are the same. There is no outer world separate from the inner world.

From the beginning of the next paragraph, which starts with "Behold your Friend, the Christ Who stands beside you," something quite different happens. It is almost as if the brass of the Course's orchestra stood up to announce this new section, reminiscent of a phrase that occurs later in the text, "the trumpet of eternity." I think you could almost see Jesus, as the conductor, pointing to the trumpets to stand up and announce this sentence. What is particularly interesting is that near the end of the text, in "The Savior's Vision," Jesus does something very similar. We turn to that section now.

The Savior's Vision

The third paragraph on page 617 begins with the sentence, "Behold your role within the universe!"; and we can see the exact same musical phrase we found in "The Lifting of the Veil": "Behold your Friend, the Christ Who stands beside you." Here, it announces the culmination and climax of the entire text. From this point to the end we find a different coloration and feeling to the writing. I should mention, by the way, that this entire section is in blank verse; in fact, about the last sixty pages of the text are in blank verse. This finale to the text can also be likened to what in music is called a coda, which comes at the end of a symphony or a large orchestral work, and departs from the usual developmental sequence of the preceding music; and that is what we find here. Not only does this section parallel in structure the final passages of "The Obstacles to Peace," but it also expresses the same theme: our role in this world of forgiveness, which brings us to the gate of Heaven.

Behold your role within the universe! To every part of true creation has the Lord of Love and Life entrusted all salvation from the misery of hell.

That is the role which the Holy Spirit has given us in this world; indeed it is the only role that we have, and a role which we share with all people: forgiveness. And it is that forgiveness that saves us from the misery of the guilt in our mind, which is the misery of hell.

And to each one has He allowed the grace to be a savior to the holy ones especially entrusted to his care.

The section in Chapter 25 called "The Special Function" makes the same point in greater detail. Each of us in this world has certain people entrusted to us, just as we are entrusted to them, with whom we learn our lessons of forgiveness. These would be the families that we are born into, the families that we establish later on, our close friends, people with whom we work, etc. And we become saviors to them just as they become our saviors, because, to say it once again, through the process of joining and forgiveness we are able to be saved from the guilt that is in our mind.

And this he learns when first he looks upon one brother as he looks upon himself, and sees the mirror of himself in him.

Another theme we find repeated throughout the Course is the idea that, by judging against them, we should not see people as different from us. Repeatedly we are exhorted not to judge each other, for when we judge we are seeing differences. The only judgment that we can make is the judgment that sees we are all the same. And we are all the same both on the basic level of sharing the same Christ, the same spiritual Identity, and we are all the same in sharing the ego belief in separation.

Thus is the concept of himself laid by, for nothing stands between his sight and what he looks upon, to judge what he beholds.

Earlier in this chapter there is a discussion of self concept versus Self. The concept of the self that we all establish is that of being separate and a victim. When that concept is changed, which we do through forgiveness, there are no ego interferences that stand between us and the other person. This again is the central teaching of the Course: If we truly looked upon each other without projections of guilt, sin or fear, then all we would see is a mirror of who we really are: the face of Christ, the vision of innocence.

And in this single vision does he see the face of Christ, and understands he looks on everyone as he beholds this one.

That is what the Course means in other sections when it says when we totally forgive one person we are forgiving all, because we are all the same. We are all the same in our vision when we see through the eyes of holiness, because there is nothing within us that would interfere with the extension of the Holy Spirit's vision. Therefore, the method the Course presents to us is to undo all the interferences that we place between ourselves and each other. We do not have to worry about what we would see or what we should do. We simply let go of the interferences to this vision, or the obstacles to peace, and then automatically we will follow the Holy Spirit's guidance.

For there is light where darkness was before, and now the veil is lifted from his sight.

The light of forgiveness replaces the darkness of the projected guilt and that is what lifts the veil. Once again, our purpose is not to seek after God, — our purpose is simply to remove the obstacles to the experience of Him. Next we see practically a direct quotation of the obstacles.

The veil across the face of Christ, the fear of God and of salvation, and the love of guilt and death, they all are different names for just one error (the love of guilt and death refers specifically to the first and third obtacles, and we could certainly throw in the second obstacle too, the attraction of pain); **that there is a space between you and your brother, kept apart by an illusion of yourself that holds him off from you, and you away from him.**

If we look again at Chart B, we can understand this passage as saying that the various obstacles — all that concerns us in the upper part of the right-hand box — are but different names or symbols for the one basic error of separation. This error — the belief there is a space between us — is the little gap that we have talked about before. It is the belief that we are separate, which comes from the projection of the original belief that we had separated from God. This belief automatically separates us from the Christ in us, and then gets projected out resulting in the belief that we are indeed separate from the Christ in our brothers and sisters. And all of this, as we have seen, "protects" us from the nonexistent wrath of God, which itself is the ego's protection against God's Love.

The sword of judgment is the weapon that you give to the illusion of yourself, that it may fight to keep the space that holds your brother off unoccupied by love.

Continually we use judgment to keep ourselves separate from each other, and the Course is asking us not to judge. I think that would be a wonderful way of summarizing what the basic undoing would be. It is consistently judging that keeps us separate. Moreover, there is no way we could ever judge anything because there is no way we could know or understand anything. We must let go of judgment. Furthermore, the only one who judges truly is the Holy Spirit. Referring to Chart B, bottom of the right-hand side, the basic fear is the fear of God's love. So what the ego is always trying to do is to split us off from this place of love in us, and then obviously to split us off from the place of love in our brothers. Judging is a form of attack and a form of fear, and once we judge and attack, then the memory of God's Love must be obscured to us.

Yet while you hold this sword, you must perceive the body as yourself, for you are bound to separation from the sight of him who holds the mir-

ror to another view of what he is, and thus what you must be.

We believe that we are separate as long as we perceive that we are a body, because bodies are separate. Minds are joined but bodies cannot join. Skip over now to the bottom of page 619, in the opening lines of the final section "Choose Once Again," where the same point is made.

Temptation has one lesson it would teach, in all its forms, wherever it occurs. It would persuade the holy Son of God he is a body, born in what must die, unable to escape its frailty, and bound by what it orders him to feel.

One of the key pronouncements in the Course is that we are not bodies, and that God did not create us as bodies. There is that recurring theme in the workbook, where one whole review is based on it: "I am not a body. I am free. For I am still as God created me." God created us as spirit, and spirit is total unity. We substituted the ego, the belief in separation, which we then projected out into a body, and whenever we judge someone as being different from us, obviously then, we are judging his body which becomes then the judgment of our own. And at that point, we can never discern the reality of who that person is. That judgment then becomes a veil across the face of Christ. Let us return now to where we left off on page 618, first paragraph.

What is temptation but the wish to stay in hell and misery? And what could this give rise to but

an image of yourself that can be miserable, and remain in hell and torment? Who has learned to see his brother not as this has saved himself, and thus is he a savior to the rest.

That temptation is to judge and see ourselves and others as being a body. When we judge someone else, obviously we are judging ourselves and that makes us miserable and in constant pain. So if we think of that workbook lesson, "When I am healed I am not healed alone," it means when our mind is healed then Jesus or the Holy Spirit extends that healing through us to the whole Sonship.

To everyone has God entrusted all, because a partial savior would be one who is but partly saved.

That is why we are repeatedly asked not to deny the unity of Christ in anyone, thus not to omit or exclude anyone in the entire universe from the Sonship of God. This means if I have forgiven you but have not forgiven someone else, then I have not truly forgiven you either. There would still be some aspect of guilt that I am holding onto, and even though that may not be directly manifested in my relationship with you, that guilt is still in my mind. If you think of a funnel, and there are still some spots of guilt at the neck of the funnel, then that would automatically have to be projected out. And I may not directly experience that with you, but if there is someone else that I am holding a grievance against, then on some level I am holding it against you as well.

The holy ones whom God has given each of you to save are everyone you meet or look upon, not knowing who they are; all those you saw an instant and forgot, and those you knew a long while since, and those you will yet meet; the unremembered and the not yet born. For God has given you His Son to save from every concept that he ever held.

Everyone who comes across our path, everyone who walks across this screen of our lives onto whom we project the ego belief system, each of these is Christ but we do not see them as Christ. Rather we see them as we would want them to be. The word "concept" here refers back to the self concept discussed on page 610, which is an ego concept of an ego. The Son whom God has given us is not only Jesus, as may be misinterpreted if a person is reading this casually, the Son is everyone.

Yet while you wish to stay in hell, how could you be the savior of the Son of God?

As long as we choose to remain within the hell of the ego's thought system, to believe that we are sinful and guilty, there is no way that we could be an extension of that forgiveness to others. So the choice is not only what we would see in another person, but always what we would see in ourselves.

For holiness is seen through holy eyes that look upon the innocence within, and thus expect to see it everywhere.

This is the same principle the Course states elsewhere: projection makes perception. First we look within, and what we see within is what we will project outward. If we look within and see sin, then that is what is projected onto our brothers and sisters, and we perceive sin in them. If, however, we look within and see the innocence of Christ, then it is that innocence which becomes extended by the Holy Spirit in us. What is important here is that in no way does this have anything to do with what our physical eyes see or do not see. We could be living in the midst of Nazi Germany, or any form of oppression or injustice, and yet still be able to see holiness in all peoples — not because there is anything out there on the level of form that is holy, but rather that the inner holiness of Christ is seen in our brothers and sisters, a holiness which now becomes a mirror of our own.

And so they call it forth in everyone they look upon, that he may be what they expect of him. This is the savior's vision; that he see his innocence in all he looks upon, and sees his own salvation everywhere.

Q: So from the point of view of the Course is this what true power is, being able to see that innocence everywhere?

A: That is the only power, the power of Christ in this world, which the world would call weakness. In the ego's world everything is interpreted upside down, and what is weak is seen as powerful, and what is truly strength is seen as weakness. The savior's vision is what the whole purpose of the Course is about, and that is what enables us to get through that final veil, that final obstacle. It is realizing that this one person whom we have made into the arch enemy is truly our friend, and therefore he or she is our savior.

Moreover, the strength of Christ totally frees us from any dependence upon anything or anyone in the world. In that sense it gives us absolute power because we realize we are in control of everything we perceive as happening to us; *not* on the level of form or the body, but on the level of our perceptions of what appears to be happening to us. And that is what literally gives us power over the world. That is what Jesus meant when he said on page 51 of the text: "In this world you need not have tribulation because I have overcome the world. That is why you should be of good cheer." Jesus overcame the world through the power of the Christ in him, even unto overcoming death, and he shares that power with all of us.

Q: Why does a lot of spiritual literature caution us not to get caught up in seeking power?

A: Clearly in the context you are referring to, power is given to things of the world. Some people say do not get caught up in the temptations of the flesh, money or fame because then we will give them power over us. As a result we are taught that we have to separate ourselves from those forms. The Course, on the other hand, says that we do not separate ourselves from the forms because the forms are not the problem; we separate from our perception of the forms, or the ego's perception of the forms. In essence, the savior's vision is total freedom from the world's dominion over us, no matter what the world would seem to do. That is why the Course is so emphatic in teaching that we are not victims; the moment that we see ourselves as victims of someone else, we are giving that person power over us.

He holds no concept of himself between his calm and open eyes and what he sees.

There is no barrier now between what we perceive outside and what we have perceived inside. There is no difference between the inner and the outer, there is just an even and easy flow back and forth. Remember that the key element in the ego system, in terms of its whole defensive structure, is that the world out there is separate and independent from us and, moreover, has power over us. The savior's vision is realizing that there is no difference between the inner and the outer. What I perceive and experience within is what I perceive and experience without.

He brings the light to what he looks upon, that he may see it as it really is.

Regardless of the forms of darkness the world calls sinful or evil, we still see the light shining because we bring the light with us. When Jesus walked the earth there was light all around him because there was only light within him, and that is what he saw. He only perceived light. On the cross he understood the veils of darkness that people placed over that light, but his vision went right through the veil to the light which was hidden. And that would be the Holy Spirit's judgment: seeing the expression of hatred as being fear, which is really a call for love or, in this context, a call for the light. That is what enables us to pass beyond that final veil.

The ego would teach us that that veil over the fear of God, the final obstacle, is solid and inpenetrable, and no light could ever get through. As we have seen, however, what changes is not the veil — what the ego has told us is the problem — what changes is our vision. It is almost as though we become like Superman, with X-ray vision that looks beyond the seeming solidity, realizing that what seemed impervious to change was really nothing, just a flimsy little veil that sought to hide the light of Christ and which now disappears. This is the savior's vision that enables us to lift that final veil.

Whatever form temptation seems to take, it always but reflects a wish to be a self that you are not.

No matter what the form of temptation we would identify in our experience, if we honestly evaluate it, we would realize that all temptation is to be *not* as God created us, i.e., that we are an ego, a body that the world has victimized.

And from that wish (which is the basic wish to be

separate from God and to make that a reality) **a concept rises, teaching that you are the thing you wish to be.**

As has been explained earlier, we construct a self we believe is the innocent victim of what has been done to it. We believe we have victimized God, a belief which we project, so now it seems that He victimizes us. Thus we are in a body, trapped in this victimizing world we have projected, which ultimately we believe is the product of the Will of this avenging God.

It will remain your concept of yourself until the wish that fathered it no longer is held dear.

So the problem is not the self we believe we are, this innocent victim that is hurt by the world. The problem is the underlying wish that set up the separation situation, and has nothing to do with any of our dreams of victimhood — anything relating to our body or the bodies of others, our special relationships. The problem always goes back to the original instant when we chose to see ourselves as separate.

But while you cherish it (while you cherish a belief in separation, identifying as an ego instead of Christ), **you will behold your brother in the likeness of the self whose image has the wish begot of you.**

As long as we identify as an ego, then that is what we project out, seeing our brothers and sisters as egos; but what we see in them is simply the mirror of what we have done to ourselves. We see ourselves as a separated body because that is what we have wished for and chosen; and therefore that is what we project and see in someone else.

For seeing can but represent a wish, because it has no power to create.

This is an indirect statement of the Atonement principle. Only the ego wishes and makes illusions, and God and His Son will and create reality. However, in the illusion it appears as if we are free to believe, wish and choose anything that we like, and our perceptions arise out of that through projection. Nevertheless, projection cannot make reality an illusion, and it cannot make illusion a reality. Wishing has had no effect on the truth, since it cannot create, but only make the ephemeral.

Yet it can look with love or look with hate, depending only on the simple choice of whether you would join with what you see, or keep yourself apart and separate.

Everything comes down to that same basic choice. If we think back to what we have discussed about the messengers of fear and the messengers of love, the problem is always which messenger we have chosen to send out: not the messages that are brought back to us, but the messages that we have asked the messenger for.

The savior's vision is as innocent of what your

brother is as it is free of any judgment made upon yourself. It sees no past in anyone at all. And thus it serves a wholly open mind, unclouded by old concepts, and prepared to look on only what the present holds.

This would be an expression of what the Course calls the "holy instant." That is the instant when the savior's vision is extended. And it is a vision and an instant when there is no past; no guilt or sin of the past, no fear of the future. There is simply the forgiveness and love of the present. The process starts with "a little willingness," which is then built upon. But we cannot do this alone without the help of the Holy Spirit. Our job is simply to question what we have made real, and to truly desire something else.

It cannot judge because it does not know. And recognizing this, it merely asks, "What is the meaning of what I behold?" Then is the answer given.

So the savior's vision, devoid of judgment, asks to be told the meaning of what it beholds. As we ask for the corrected perception of the Holy Spirit, what we behold becomes some expression of forgiveness, some expression of joining. But we are not the ones who give the answer. The answer is given us by the Holy Spirit. We simply clear away all the obstacles to that answer. Basically the four obstacles to peace merely represent a process of undoing; bringing the obstacle to the love that is underneath it, and then love shines it away.

**And the door held open for the face of Christ to
shine upon the one who asks, in innocence, to
see beyond the veil of old ideas and ancient concepts held so long and dear against the vision of
the Christ in you.**

Q: I am wondering if I understand the process
described here correctly. Is it the idea that first we
will be tempted to see with the body's eyes and
make a judgment, and then being aware of that
constantly, we can ask what is the meaning of
what I behold?

A: Right. That really is what the process is. Very
often we are confronted by situations in our lives
that seem to have no resolution. Because of the
amount of our hurt, fear, guilt and anxiety, it all
seems so overwhelming. Perhaps there will be a
situation that we really want solved, and it seems
that no matter what we do it is not going to work
out. It is as if there were a stalemate. In these
cases all that is asked of us is simply to remember
to bring to the Holy Spirit or Jesus all our temptations to see or feel the situation according to the
"old ideas and ancient concepts held so long";
and then as openly and honestly as we can, turn
it over to Him and say: not my way, but Thine be
done.

This presupposes, of course, that we have no
investment in the outcome whatsoever. To the extent that we have none, the answer will be given
us. And that is how the door referred to in the
above passage is held open. We do not open the
door. In a sense, we just express a willingness to

have the door be opened for us. And we will know the truth of what we have received if we see this person whom we hated transformed to someone whom we love. As it says in "For They Have Come" in Chapter 26: "The holiest of all the spots on earth is where an ancient hatred has become a present love." When the word "ancient" appears, incidentally, it usually comes within a section that has a different feeling tone, just as we find here. In fact the word "ancient" is used more often than any other in "For They Have Come," which I think is the most beautiful section in the entire Course. It catapults you away from the very narrow band of human experience to a much deeper dimension, that ancient instant before this world began.

Be vigilant against temptation, then, remembering that it is but a wish, insane and meaningless, to make yourself a thing that you are not.

The temptation would always be experienced or expressed in some form that would see us as separate from another person. It comes from that one insane wish that made this world to begin with, and keeps it going.

And think as well upon the thing that you would be instead. It is a thing of madness, pain and death; a thing of treachery and black despair, of failing dreams and no remaining hope except to die, and end the dream of fear.

This is talking about the physical and psychological body, the self concept, and everything that the ego is. It certainly is a concise description of the world we made.

***This* is temptation; nothing more than this. Can this be difficult to choose *against*?**

Think back to the last sentence in Chapter 23: "Who with the Love of God upholding him could find the choice of miracles or murder hard to make?" The idea is that we have to realize that we are being upheld by the Love of God and not the fear of the ego. At that point we can clearly see what the choice is, and it is always between the miracle and murder, forgiveness and a grievance, love and hatred. The difficulty, as always, is that we are not aware that that is the choice, because the ego has made a myriad number of smoke screens which confuse us about what the issue really is. The temptation is not to fight back in the belief that we are unfairly treated, or despairingly to destroy our personal world; nor is it to make a great deal of money, attain sexual conquests, or to achieve status and fame. The temptation is but to see ourself as a body, an ego self, because that is what keeps away from us the loving memory of God.

Consider what temptation is, and see the real alternatives you choose between. There are but two. Be not deceived by what appears as many choices. There is hell or Heaven, and of these you choose but one.

This is a constant theme in all three books. The ego world seems to offer us many, many different choices. The ego never informs us that none of its choices is real. Turning to page 607, "The Real Alternative," we read from the last paragraph of the page.

Real choice is no illusion. But the world has none to offer. All its roads but lead to disappointment, nothingness and death. There is no choice in its alternatives. Seek not escape from problems here. The world was made that problems could not *be* escaped. Be not deceived by all the different names its roads are given. They have but one end. And each is but the means to gain that end, for it is here that all its roads will lead, however differently they seem to start; however differently they seem to go. Their end is certain, for there is no choice among them. All of them will lead to death.

This is a very powerful section. It spells out clearly how there are no choices in this world because the world was made to keep the real choice away from us. This is a recurring theme in the book. The only choice we ever have is that between hell or Heaven, a grievance or forgiveness, murder or the miracle — there is nothing else. During any given situation we could choose to see through the eyes of the ego, the eyes of attack, separation and death; or we could choose to see through the eyes of Christ, a way of seeing which apprehends all situations as an opportunity of joining with our brother or sister.

Let us return to the paragraph closing the section on page 619.

Let not the world's light, given unto you, be hidden from the world. It needs the light, for it is dark indeed, and men despair because the savior's vision is withheld and what they see is death.

This idea is similar to the gospel statement where Jesus says, "Do not hide your light under a bushel"; rather we are to bring the light into the open and let it shine. This idea is amplified in the manual which talks about the "plan of the teachers." Turning to the bottom of page 1 in the manual, we read:

Everyone who follows the world's curriculum, and everyone here does follow it until he changes his mind, teaches solely to convince himself that he is what he is not. Herein is the purpose of the world. What else, then, would its curriculum be? Into this hopeless and closed learning situation, which teaches nothing but despair and death, God sends His teachers. And as they teach His lessons of joy and hope, their learning finally becomes complete.

Except for God's teachers there would be little hope of salvation, for the world of sin would seem forever real.

Therefore the purpose of the Course is to help prepare more and more people, more and more quickly, to be that shining light that will go into the world: the world being a place of darkness and death in which people despair because they see nothing else. Our function is to be that light.

Please do not misread this and lay a guilt trip on yourself by believing that as long as you withhold that vision then the world will see death. Rather the Course is saying that people are patiently waiting for us. Just as it also says in the manual, when the teacher is ready he sends out a light and then his pupils find him. This is saying the same thing. There are people who are just waiting for us to change our minds and be that light. As we become that light, through forgiveness, then that light shines out to more people. As that process increases, the circle of Atonement widens and extends, and more and more people are brought into the healing nature of this light. We return to page 619, second paragraph.

Their savior stands, unknowing and unknown, beholding them with eyes unopened.

"The Lifting of the Veil" talks about the "knowing and known," and here we find the opposite, the "unknowing and unknown." The saviors of the world, which is each of us, stand among all people and yet, because of our own choice to hold onto guilt and our belief in the body and separation, we do not know who we are (The Christ), and people do not know us either.

And they cannot see (our brothers who have chosen us) **until he** (i.e., the savior) **looks on them with seeing eyes, and offers them forgiveness with his own. Can you to whom God says, "Release My Son!" be tempted not to listen, when you learn that it is you for whom He asks re-**

**lease? And what but this is what this course
would teach? And what but this is there for you
to learn?**

If we understand the Course message, each and
every time we are confronted by a situation in a
relationship that tempts us to see separation and
judgment, and to make them real, we will be able
to hear Jesus speak God's words to us: "Release
My Son!" Thus we realize that the Son who is
released is not only our brother and sister, but is
also ourselves. At that point how can we not listen, how can we not do what he asks of us? Very
simply Jesus is urging us to do what he says because it will make us feel better. By making us feel
better, our listening to Jesus will automatically
make others feel better, too.

The key idea, once again, is that whatever I do
to you, I do to myself. What I do to myself, I do to
you. Salvation for you means salvation for me,
and vice versa. In this sense only, the salvation of
the world rests upon the decisions that God's
teachers make. From that lofty perspective, the
purpose of the Course is to help more and more
people realize that they are God's teachers, and
that their own healing will come as they become
instruments of healing.

Before we return to the final obstacle, let us turn
to the middle of page 413 in the text, in case we
are tempted to take this dream much too seriously.

**What if you recognized this world is an halluci-
nation? What if you really understood you made**

271

it up? What if you realized that those who seem to walk about in it, to sin and die, attack and murder and destroy themselves, are wholly unreal? . . .

Hallucinations disappear when they are recognized for what they are. This is the healing and the remedy. Believe them not and they are gone. And all you need to do is recognize that *you* did this.

If we really can integrate this teaching, and remember that the entire drama of our lives is literally an hallucination, practicing the Course would be much easier. In fact we would not take things as seriously as we do: For example, if we are caught in the middle of a very heavy ego attack, remembering that this is an hallucination we made up might relieve some of our tension, anger or fear.

The Lifting of the Veil (concl.)

Now we are going to finish the final obstacle to peace, returning to the second paragraph on page 394, the trumpets standing up and proclaiming:

Behold your Friend, the Christ Who stands beside you.

This is the culmination of the four obstacles, and the means by which we finally pass beyond the veil. We realize that this person standing next to us is not the enemy, is not the devil. It is our Friend with a capital "F," meaning this is our brother and sister in Christ.

How holy and beautiful He is! You thought He sinned because you cast the veil of sin upon Him to hide His loveliness.

A similarity in feeling tone can be sensed here with that in the section "For They Have Come," which begins, "Think but how holy you must be from whom the Voice for God calls lovingly unto your brother. . . ." We thought others had sinned against us because we projected our sin upon them.

Yet still He holds forgiveness out to you, to share His holiness. This "enemy," this "stranger" still offers you salvation as His Friend. The "enemies" of Christ, the worshippers of sin, know not Whom they attack.

All the pronouns here are capitalized to emphasize that this Brother standing next to us is the
Christ. He is Christ because we are Christ and we
are One.

**This is your brother, crucified by sin and wait-
ing for release from pain.**

Others are crucified by what they believe are
their sins, and we are not responsible for their
crucifixion, or their own belief in being separate.
Yet they are waiting for release from their pain
because they cannot do it themselves. And we
cannot do it ourselves either. As we saw at the top
of page 394, "And you will raise your eyes in faith
together, or not at all."

**Would you not offer him forgiveness, when only
he can offer it to you? For his redemption he will
give you yours, as surely as God created every
living thing and loves it. And he will give it
truly, for it will be both offered and received.**

The same motifs are brought back over and over
again in this great symphonic structure. We have
just seen how "The Savior's Vision," in Chapter
31, emphasized the same idea of our mutual redemption. Many times however, our experience
does not seem to validate this mutual healing. For
example, there is someone whom we have hated
and then forgiven; someone who may be physically sick and we ask for corrected perception to
see that person differently; and yet nothing external seems to shift. Nonetheless, this passage is
saying that if we offer forgiveness and healing it

must be received, even if the person has not consciously done so. The sections on healing in the manual specifically address this issue.

There is no grace of Heaven that you cannot offer ⸺ **to one another, and receive from your most holy Friend. Let him withhold it not, for by receiving it you offer it to him. Redemption has been given you to give each other, and thus receive it. Whom you forgive is free, and what you give you share. Forgive the sins your brother thinks he has committed, and all the guilt you think you see in him.**

The important point here, made many other times, is that to give the gift of forgiveness and love, the gift of Christ, is how we make it our own. As Jesus says in the closing pages of the text: "To give this gift is how to make it yours. And God ordained, in loving kindness, that it be for you." Giving and receiving are the same. This passage also parallels the scriptural statement, cited often in the Course and discussed earlier, in which Jesus says to the apostles: "Those whose sins you forgive are forgiven, and those whose sins you bind, are bound." Each of us has that ⸺ power to have our mind healed and extend that healing to others, or to imprison our minds and thereby reinforce the imprisonment for the other person.

From here to the end of the section, as I already noted, we find a strong Easter theme running throughout. The message of Easter is the message of lilies, the flower of Easter, and for the Course lilies are a symbol of forgiveness. The message of Easter is the message that Jesus taught us from the cross: Nothing in this world has power over us, or can keep us separated from each other or from the God Who created us. Thus, standing before the veil reflects our decision to join with Jesus' resurrection or crucifixion. Choosing the resurrection is our choice for the total forgiveness that undoes sin, and which enables us to move beyond the veil and overcome that final obstacle. That is what Jesus taught us from the cross because, by not seeing sin at all but only calls for help, he forgave the sins that the world could never have forgiven. Thus the holy place of resurrection he refers to here is that place mentioned on page 393: "And it is here you choose whether to look upon it or wander on, only to return and make the choice again."

Here is the holy place of resurrection, to which we come again; to which we will return until redemption is accomplished and received.

The message eloquently expressed by Jesus is: "Please forgive now and let us be done with it; if you withhold forgiveness you will only have to return. Whatever it is you cannot forgive in this one person, whom you have made the symbol of the devil, you will eventually have to forgive until redemption is accomplished. Please, let me help you look at this person differently. Do what I did, and I will be with you to help you do it."

Think who your brother is, before you would condemn him.

The idea is not only to think of who he is, the Christ, but also to remember that the way we see him is the way we see ourselves.

And offer thanks to God that he is holy, and has been given the gift of holiness for you. Join him in gladness, and remove all trace of guilt from his disturbed and tortured mind. Help him to lift the heavy burden of sin you laid upon him and he accepted as his own, and toss it lightly and with happy laughter away from him. Press it not like thorns against his brow, nor nail him to it, unredeemed and hopeless.

Jesus is here using the symbols of the crucifixion — the crown of thorns and the nails. The crucifixion is the Course's symbol of the ego — the symbol of all the beliefs we have that we are victimized, so that we victimize in return — and we are being asked to change our attitude and look at everything differently: "lightly and with happy laughter." We are not responsible for the crown of thorns that other people wear. All we are responsible for is our belief that it *is* a crown of thorns, which reinforces the belief that the other is wearing a crown of thorns. In that sense we have pressed that crown of thorns even more tightly against the person's brow. That belief is our responsibility, and if we look beyond what those thorns symbolize, realizing that they are calls for help, we will see the Christ that is in that person. Then the crown is lifted. The ultimate meaning of the crucifixion is the belief in separation, and if I do not see you separate from me, then you are not separate from me.

Give faith to one another, for faith and hope and mercy are yours to give.

This is the faith — regardless of what the ego sees, no matter how many veils of darkness are placed between ourselves — that still knows the light of Christ shines in our brother or sister. That certainty of Christ that passes beyond the ego appearances is the meaning of faith. This statement, by the way, is taken from the famous Pauline teaching of faith, hope and charity (or love); here the word mercy is substituted.

Into the hands that give, the gift is given. Look on your brother, and see in him the gift of God you would receive. It is almost Easter, the time of resurrection. Let us give redemption to each other and share in it, that we may rise as one in resurrection, not separate in death.

What we give to others is what we receive. The resurrection is the choice that Jesus made, and now it is the choice that he is helping us to make as well. We cannot make it until we believe that we are better off in doing it, knowing that by freeing someone from the belief in sin and separation we are freeing ourselves.

Behold the gift of freedom that I gave the Holy Spirit for both of you. And be you free together, as you offer to the Holy Spirit this same gift. And giving it, receive it of Him in return for what you gave. He leadeth you and me together (that is from the Psalms), **that we might meet here in this holy place, and make the same decision.**

The Lifting of the Veil [concl.]

We can understand from this statement that Jesus walks the same path with us. It is a path he took and that he makes each and every time we choose to let him accompany us. The same idea is expressed in the introduction to the Fifth Review in the workbook, near the top of page 322.

I take the journey with you. For I share your doubts and fears a little while, that you may come to me who recognize the road by which all fears and doubts are overcome. We walk together. I must understand uncertainty and pain, although I know they have no meaning. Yet a savior must remain with those he teaches, seeing what they see, but still retaining in his mind the way that led him out, and now will lead you out with him. God's Son is crucified until you walk along the road with me.
My resurrection comes again each time I lead a brother safely to the place at which the journey ends and is forgot.

This is the same place we are talking about here in "The Lifting of the Veil": standing before this final obstacle.

I am renewed each time a brother learns there is a way from misery and pain. I am reborn each time a brother's mind turns to the light in him and looks for me. I have forgotten no one. Help me now to lead you back to where the journey was begun, to make another choice with me.

Jesus is saying in the review exactly what he is saying here, asking each of us to walk that same

path that he walked; not literally through a crucifixion but through the meaning of the crucifixion
— the temptation to see ourselves unfairly treated
by the world — and then to change our perception and join the resurrection. This especially ap-
plies when we feel victimized by the one person
we have chosen to be the symbol of the world's
evil, which is nothing more than the projection of
the evil we believe is inside of us. Remember that
what makes this process possible is knowing that
we are not alone. As Jesus said in that workbook
passage, he has "forgotten no one." All that is
required when we are confronted by a situation or
relationship that brings up confusion, hurt and
pain, is to know that he is with us. Then we can
turn to him and ask for help. That "little willingness" is the only thing he asks of us.

Return now to page 395 in the text.

**Free your brother here, as I freed you. Give
him the self-same gift, nor look upon him with
condemnation of any kind.**

The same love and freedom that we would accept from Jesus is the same love and freedom that
he would ask us to extend to another. We are talking here about an experience of complete forgiveness.

**See him as guiltless as I look on you, and over-
look the sins he thinks he sees within himself.**

If people have done something that we have
judged as unconscionable and horrendous, it is
only because they have seen sin within them-

selves and have projected it onto us or someone else. Just as we would like Jesus to look only upon the innocence in us and beyond all our seeming sins, that is what he is asking us to do with our brother or sister.

Offer your brother freedom and complete release from sin, here in the garden of seeming agony and death.

There is a reference earlier in the text in Chapter 6 when, talking about his own last days, Jesus speaks about the "agony in the garden" and it is put in quotes. This indicates that there was no agony in the garden, although down the centuries it has become another way of trying to make Jesus into one who suffered conflict and pain. This world seems to be a garden of agony and death, because that is how we made it. In reality, of course, it is nothing. Earlier, the text speaks about the seeming terror that the Holy Spirit would help us walk through. This final obstacle, because it is so close to what the ego has taught us is the fear of God and His punishment, is in truth only the ego's fear of a God of Love. As the unconscious guilt and self-hatred begin to surface in awareness we experience agony and pain. It becomes a learning opportunity, if we but look at it with Jesus or the Holy Spirit. As he said in the preceding page, we could "toss it lightly and with happy laughter away," realizing that it is nothing.

So will we prepare together the way unto the res-

urrection of God's Son, and let him rise again to glad remembrance of his Father, Who knows no sin, no death, but only life eternal.

It is obvious in this passage that Jesus is not talking about his own resurrection, but the resurrection within each of us that is the awakening from the dream of death. What he did he is now asking all of us to do as well.

Together we will disappear into the Presence beyond the veil, not to be lost but found; not to be seen but known. And knowing, nothing in the plan God has established for salvation will be left undone.

Together with Jesus, and joined with the brother or sister whom we have made to be our greatest obstacle, we will finally disappear into the Presence of Christ and God beyond the veil, no longer lost in the ego's world, but found. Just as in the parable of "The Lost Sheep," the shepherd will leave the ninety-nine sheep to find the one who is lost. It is the same idea here.

"Seeing" occurs within the world of perception; being "known" is the synonym for Heaven, or the awareness of oneness with God and all creation. This is when we see the face of Christ in our brother and remember God. "And knowing (being in awareness of God and Heaven), nothing in the plan God has established for salvation will be left undone." At that point we will look on everything differently, knowing that what God has ordained has never not been. As Jesus says earlier in the text, "The outcome is as certain as God."

This is the journey's purpose, without which is the journey meaningless.

This world is essentially without meaning until we recognize that its only purpose is to learn forgiveness. It is realizing that this is its only purpose that makes everything in the world meaningful. However cruel, purposeless, or meaningless our lives might seem to be, our recognition of why we chose to come here pulls together all the seemingly separated fragments of our own experience into one meaningful whole.

Here is the peace of God, given to you eternally by Him. Here is the rest and quiet that you seek, the reason for the journey from its beginning.

You could think of this as the individual journeys that we believe we are on in our individual lifetimes, as well as the greater journey of the carpet of time that originated with the belief that we were separate, and which will finally end when every last person remembers who he or she really is.

Heaven is the gift you owe your brother, the debt of gratitude you offer to the Son of God in thanks for what he is, and what his Father created him to be.

When the Course talks about the gift we owe each other, the debt of gratitude, it is not within the connotation of the world. It is simply a poetic and stylistic way of saying this is the gift that we should give each other, because it is the gift that we should give ourselves. When the workbook states, "Love is the way I walk in gratitude," we find the same idea. The spirit of gratitude for what our relationships really are, for who our brothers and sisters really are, is what enables us to remember that God is Love and that we are created like Him.

Think carefully how you would look upon the giver of this gift, for as you look on him so will the gift itself appear to be. As he is seen as either the giver of guilt or salvation, so will his offering be seen and so received.

The way that I *choose* to see you — as someone who either reinforces my guilt and separation, or someone who offers me salvation — is, in the final analysis, the way that I *will* see you. It has nothing to do with what your behavior or form is, because projection makes perception. If my consciousness is one of self-hatred or guilt — whether deeply repressed or in awareness — then, by the law of projection, that is what I will automatically perceive in you and the world around me.

The crucified give pain because they are in pain. But the redeemed give joy because they have been healed of pain.

If in consciousness I perceive myself as being crucified, as being victimized by the world, then there is no way that I could avoid wanting to crucify that world. If I know that I am forgiven and redeemed, then it is that same forgiveness and joy that I would offer, extend and give to you. There is certainly no more joyous or happy experience in this world than to truly know and experience that our sins are forgiven. Since the source of all our unhappiness is believing that we are guilty and sinful, to have even a brief moment when we suddenly realize that we are truly loved by God, and that nothing has happened to change that, is the most joyous moment in the world.

Joy comes from the realization that we are redeemed, and the pain of our guilt vanishes because it has been healed through forgiveness. The occurrence is not a cognitive or intellectual event. Rather it is an experience of the sudden realization, in the midst of the darkness that we believe is so real inside of us, that there is a light that is shining that has never stopped shining. And so our sins have disappeared into the nothingness from which they came. Basically, joy simply means that we were wrong and God was right.

Everyone gives as he receives, but he must choose what it will *be* that he receives.

What we receive is not anything of the material world. We can only receive the joy and Love of God or the pain of the ego, as we choose. Furthermore, what I receive from you will always be what I have given you. In "The 'Dynamics' of the Ego," the bottom paragraph on page 191 we read:

Every brother you meet becomes a witness for Christ or for the ego, depending on what you perceive in him. Everyone convinces you of what you want to perceive, and of the reality of the

kingdom you have chosen for your vigilance. Everything you perceive is a witness to the thought system you want to be true. Every brother has the power to release you, if you choose to be free. You cannot accept false witness of him unless you have evoked false witnesses against him. If he speaks not of Christ to you, you spoke not of Christ to him.

If I perceive you as not being Christlike to me, it is only because I have first perceived myself as not being Christlike to you. It does not matter what you have done, no matter how heinous your sins have been against me, my family or my people. I can still see you as being a witness for Christ. And the way that I see you will tell me the way I first saw myself.

We return to "The Lifting of the Veil," and the same idea repeated.

And he will recognize his choice by what he gives, and what is given him.

Once again, the way that I can always tell what I have chosen to see in myself, the ego or Christ, is how I see you: The way that I see you is the way that I see myself.

Nor is it given anything in hell or Heaven to interfere with his decision.

The decision is unmistakably ours to make. Therefore, Jesus cannot give us what we do not want. He can hold it out to us but cannot force it on us, any more than he can remove a fear we still

cling to, as he says in Chapter 2. If I choose to see
myself as a Son of God, as a child of peace and of
love, then nothing that happens to me can ever
change that decision. That choice would always
hold regardless of what the world seems to do,
whether we are "victims" of the Holocaust or a
silly schoolyard prank. On the other hand if I
choose to see myself as a son of the ego, a child of
guilt and fear and sin, then no matter how much
love Jesus is offering to me I will not be able to
accept it. And nothing and no one can interfere
with this decision.

**You came this far because the journey was your
choice. And no one undertakes to do what he believes is meaningless.**

This idea is repeated many times throughout
the Course. Assuming that if we have come this
far in terms of understanding the text and what
the true meaning of our relationships are, then
we are that much closer to the end of the journey.
It does not necessarily mean that we will choose
to take the final step and pass through that final
veil; but if we have come this far it is because part
of us has really wanted to learn the lesson. And,
as we have already seen, this is when the going
can get rough, because the contrast between the
ego and God is no longer blurred. We believe,
again, that we are in the garden of agony and
death, and this is when we need our faith in the
Presence of Jesus or the Holy Spirit; the comfort-
ing and loving Presence that will lead us past the
veil, regardless of the terror we seem to be walking through.

What you had faith in still is faithful, and watches over you in faith so gentle yet so strong that it would lift you far beyond the veil, and place the Son of God safely within the sure protection of his Father.

We can understand this in different ways, but basically what we have faith in is the whole process of the Atonement, but we can also include in this faith in Jesus, the one who stands for the Atonement. We can thus understand this in more abstract terms as the process of the Atonement, or in a more personal way as accepting the guidance and help of Jesus, who is in charge of the Atonement and lovingly watches over us. It is a way of acknowledging that we have not come this far alone. There has always been someone helping us, and of course he will help us take this final step.

Here is the only purpose that gives this world, and the long journey through this world, whatever meaning lies in them. Beyond this, they are meaningless.

Again, this world and all the weary journeys that we take have no meaning unless we give them the meaning of learning forgiveness.

You and your brother stand together, still without conviction they have a purpose. Yet is it given you to see this purpose in your holy Friend, and recognize it as your own.

We are still standing before the veil, not having

made a final decision, as if there were still a point beyond which we were not willing to go. There remains a part of us that is not quite sure that our interests are really served through total forgiveness. And yet the choice is always ours to change our mind and not see separate interests, but true joining and complete forgiveness.

The word "Friend" here refers to the Christ in our brother or sister, the holiness of the Self that is also our own. It is the same usage that you find in the line on page 394, "Behold your Friend, the Christ Who stands beside you," as it is on the top of page 397, "Look on your risen Friend, and celebrate his holiness along with me." However, usually when "Friend" is capitalized in the Course it refers to the Holy Spirit.

Q: The second line on the top of page 395 states: "Behold the gift of freedom that I gave the Holy Spirit for both of you." What exactly is meant by "the gift of freedom"? Can you say something about that, and also what it means when Jesus says "I gave the Holy Spirit"?

A: The "gift of freedom" would be the gift of freedom from the ego; basically, it is the gift of transcending the ego which Jesus exemplified in his own crucifixion and resurrection. It is the total release from the belief in guilt and separate interests; it is the freedom from the prison house of victims and victimizers. When Jesus says that he gave that "gift to the Holy Spirit for both of you" it certainly would not only mean "for both of you," but for the whole world.

Earlier in the text Jesus states that the principle of the Atonement was given to the Holy Spirit at the moment that the separation seemed to occur, but that the plan called for that principle to be set into motion. In other words, someone had to demonstrate that the separation was only a bad dream, that there are no victims or victimizers in Heaven or on earth. By becoming a pure manifestation of God's Love in the world, Jesus showed that we did not murder God or His Love. Thus, he was the one who set the plan into motion, for he was the one who first lived out the full expression of the Atonement principle: There is no separation. The Holy Spirit thus "established Jesus as the leader in carrying out His plan" since he was the first totally ego-free person. Jesus now reaches back to help everyone else transcend his or her own ego. In that sense, on behalf of the Atonement plan Jesus gave that gift of freedom from the ego to the Holy Spirit, who then uses it by spreading it in time throughout the entire Sonship. That is the larger context of that passage. You can also interpret it as a poetic expression. One final point here: in terms of function, Jesus and the Holy Spirit are the same because They both serve as our internal Teacher.

In conclusion, in terms of the seeming hardships that occur throughout the journey, we read on page 620 of the text.

Trials are but lessons that you failed to learn presented once again, so where you made a faulty choice before you now can make a better

**one, and thus escape all pain that what you chose
before has brought to you.**

What we experience as trials are really lessons
that we did not learn before. As we near the end
of the journey and approach this last obstacle —
the fear of God, reinforced by our fear of forgiveness — these lessons will probably intensify. At
this point it would be helpful to remember that
this world is an hallucination. We chose and made
it up, and thus we cannot blame anyone else for
it. Moreover, what we experience as a trial is really an opportunity to let go of deeply buried guilt
that had not arisen into our consciousness before
we reached this stage in the journey. Passing
through this final veil is basically a transition in
consciousness. If we are able to let go of our resistance to this transition, we will be lifted to another
state where we experience ourselves as totally
new and different from what we were boxed into
before.

In summary, then, as we near the end of the
journey the fear of death becomes the strongest,
the viciousness of the ego becomes the strongest,
and that is when it is most important to remember
that there is a larger context and purpose in all of
this.

As a way of concluding "The Obstacles to
Peace" I will now read one of Helen's favorite poems, "The Place of Resurrection." This is a wonderful Easter Poem that Helen had taken down
around Easter. It includes many of the themes
that we have discussed in "The Lifting of the
Veil," combining Jesus' Easter message with the

291

urging that we share the meaning of the resurrection with all people. The poem can be found on page 99 in *The Gifts of God*.

> There is an altar that I seek. For there
> And only there can certain peace be
>   found.
> The light of holiness shines white upon
> Its cooling stillness wreathed with lilies
>   round.
> Here is the place where those who
>   thought that death
> Was lord of life must come, to learn of
>   One
> Who seemed to die, that life is lord of
>   death.
> Beside the lilies sickly dreams are gone,
> And stillness spreads a blanket over all
> Who seemed to know no rest and find no
>   peace,
> To bring the quiet and the dreamless sleep
> In which their dreaming will forever
>   cease.
> Here we awake, my brothers and myself,
> For all of us come here to find the way
> To waken from the dream of sin the world
> Was made to represent. We come to lay
> Our guilt beside the altar and step back,
> Putting illusions and mistakes aside,
> And learn before an empty tomb to see,
> He is not dead Who here was crucified.

APPENDIX

Chart A

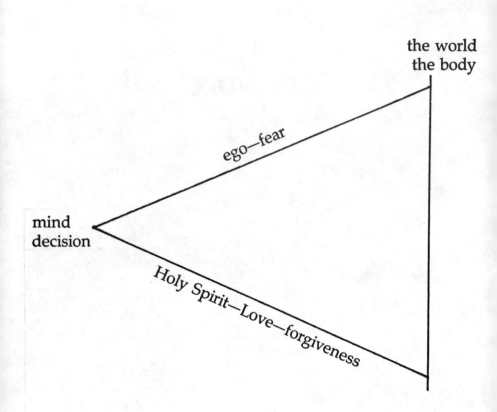

Chart B

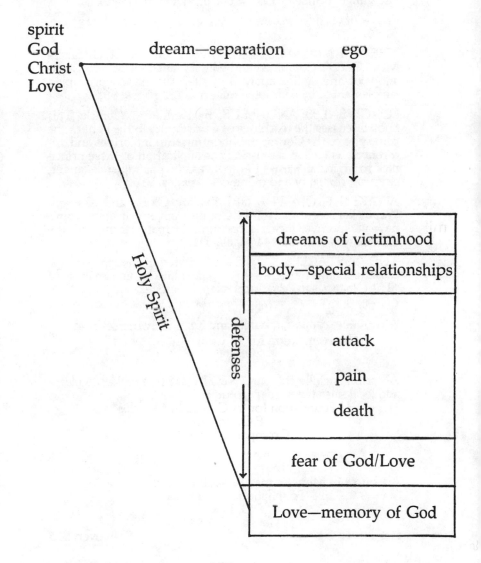

Related Material on **A Course in Miracles**

GLOSSARY-INDEX FOR "A COURSE IN MIRACLES," 2nd edition, enlarged: Summary of the Course's theory; 126 terms defined and indexed; index of over 800 scriptural references; line-gauge included to assist use of index. 312 pages. $16.

Print-out of added material to first edition; includes line gauge. $1.50.

THE FIFTY MIRACLE PRINCIPLES OF "A COURSE IN MIRACLES": Combined and edited transcript of two workshops of line by line analysis of the fifty miracle principles, supplemented by additional material. 153 pages. $8.

FORGIVENESS AND JESUS, by Kenneth Wapnick: This book discusses the teachings of Christianity in the light of the principles of the Course, highlighting the similarities and differences, as well as discussing the application of these principles to important areas in our lives such as injustice, anger, sickness, sexuality and money. 340 pages. $16.

AWAKEN FROM THE DREAM, by Gloria and Kenneth Wapnick: Presentation of the Course's major principles from a new perspective. Includes background material on how the Course was written. 144 pages. $10.

THE OBSTACLES TO PEACE: Edited transcript of tape cassette album by Kenneth Wapnick; line by line analysis of "The Obstacles to Peace" and related passages. 300 pages. $12.

A complete catalog of books and tapes is available from The Foundation for "A Course in Miracles."

All prices include shipping. New York State residents please add local sales tax. Order from:

les"

© Foundation for "A Course in Miracles"
RD #2, Box 71, Roscoe, NY 12776

A Course in Miracles may be ordered from:
Foundation for Inner Peace
P.O. Box 635
Tiburon, CA 94920

Hardcover: $40   Softcover: $25